THE PARENTS WE

THE PARENTS
WE MEAN TO BE

How Well-Intentioned Adults Undermine
Children's Moral and Emotional Development

Richard Weissbourd

HOUGHTON MIFFLIN HARCOURT
Boston • New York
2009

To my parents,

Bernard and Bernice Weissbourd

For information about permission to reproduce selections from this book, write to Permissions, Houghton Mifflin Harcourt Publishing Company, 215 Park Avenue South, New York, New York 10003.

www.hmhbooks.com

Library of Congress Cataloging-in-Publication Data
Weissbourd, Richard.
The parents we mean to be : how well-intentioned adults undermine children's moral and emotional development / Richard Weissbourd.
p. cm.
Includes bibliographical references and index.
ISBN-13: 978-0-618-62617-5
ISBN-10: 0-618-62617-4
1. Child rearing.   2. Parent and child.   3. Moral development.
I. Title.
HQ772.W365 2009
649'.7—dc22   2008036766

Printed in the United States of America

DOC 10 9 8 7 6 5 4 3 2 1

Portions of this book previously appeared in the following publications:
"Moral Teachers, Moral Students," *Education Leadership,* vol. 60, no. 6, Association for Supervision and Curriculum Development, March 2003; "Down Home," *The New Republic,* February 25, 2002; "The Feel Good Trap," *The New Republic,* Aug. 19 & 26, 1996; "Moral Parent, Moral Child," *The American Prospect,* Summer 2002; "Distancing Dad," *The American Prospect,* December 6, 1999; and *The Vulnerable Child: What Really Hurts America's Children and What We Can Do About It,* Reading, MA: Addison-Wesley, 1996.

CONTENTS

ACKNOWLEDGMENTS

Although I had been mulling over the ideas in this book for many years, it was sparked into life by a call several years ago from Deanne Urmy, my editor at Houghton Mifflin. The manuscript got steadily better because of her wisdom, superb editing, and great perseverance. But it improved perhaps most essentially because she understood deeply what was at its core and brought to it her own fine morality.

My sharp-minded, good-humored agent, Jill Kneerim, gently helped me over rough patches and is no slouch when it comes to positioning and marketing a book. Yet from the early days she pushed me to focus on how this project would be meaningful to me and contribute to the world. My great thanks to her.

My research team was simply terrific and inspiring. Shira Katz directed this project with great integrity, intelligence, and unflagging good spirits from start to finish and came through in the clutch again and again. Iva Borisova was also there from the beginning, and brought to this work keen insights and the highest moral standards. Mara Tieken joined this project midway and was fresh air—she brought new perspectives and great acuity and resourcefulness. Deborah Porter, a wise and reflective parent, conducted numerous, invaluable interviews with parents. Norma Acebedo-Rey was clear-headed and deft-minded, consistently hitting the nail on the head. Jonah Deutsch helped launch the research and conducted the first, key interviews; he also has great instincts and wisdom far beyond his years. Many thanks, too, to Abby Gegeckas, Daren Graves, Bernadette Maynard, Jennifer Oates, Melissa Steel King, and Moussie and Tara for their crucial help early on.

Thanks to my moral development group—Martha Minow, Larry Blum, and Mary Casey—for wonderful, energizing ideas and conversation and very helpful comments on numerous drafts. Tom Davey and Jake Murray, close friends, tuned into this book and got me unstuck again and again. Steven Brion-Meisels was remarkably generous and helpful. My writing group partner Gail

Caldwell understood the creation of a book at every level. In the final stages of this book, my great friend Jan Linowitz provided superb feedback and advice. Joe Finder and Michelle Souda, close friends, came through at key times. So did Robert Selman and Al Rossiter.

Ken Wapner played a vital role in this book from the beginning, offering terrific editorial advice. He focused and sharpened the book proposal and many times helped shape an argument, found a felicitous phrase, and lifted out or crystallized a key idea. Huge thanks to him.

My assistant, Judy Wasserman, was a godsend. Her kindness, resourcefulness, and efficiency made many challenging aspects of this project very easy.

I am extraordinarily lucky that among my wisest and most thoughtful readers were my own siblings, Burt, Ruth, and Bob; this book is far better because of many very illuminating conversations with them.

Many thanks to many others who offered useful comments on draft chapters:

Kyle Dodson, Michael Gillespie, Daren Graves, Nancy Hill, Delores Holmes, Will McMullen, Pam Nelson, Gil Noam, Anne Peretz, Rocco Ricci, Beverly Rimer, Katie Pakos Rimer, Laura Rogers, Pamela Seigle, Greg Dale, Michael Gillespie, Melissa Steel King, Mark Warren, Bernice Weissbourd, Donna Wick, Hiro Yoshikawa, Tom Zierk.

Many thanks to many others:

Nicole Angeloro, Mary Jo Bane, Betty Bardige, Jeff Beedy, Josh Berlin, Lynn Brown, Kristen Bub, Josh Bubar, Anne Clark, Greg Dale, William Damon, Parrish Dobson, Ben Duggan, Tara Edelshick, Kurt Fischer, Janina Fisher, Peter Fruchtman, Beth Burleigh Fuller, Michael Glenn, Michael and Patty Goldberger, Michael Goldstein, Tim and Betsy Groves, Joe, Laura, Steve, and Anna Grant, Janice Jackson, Jerome Kagan, Martha Kennedy, Kathryn Kenyon, Dan Kindlon, William Kolen, Francois Lemaire, Michael Lewis, Sara Lawrence-Lightfoot, Susan Lynn, Melissa Ludtke, Suniya Luthar,

Kevin and Louisa McCall, David Meglathery, Amy Monkiewicz, Chris Monks, Brian Moore, Rory Morton, Doug Newman, Gail Nunes, Gabriel O'Malley, Steven Mintz, Tim Otchy, Peggy Miller, Mica Pollock, Taryn Roeder, Ariela Rothstein, Chris Saheed, John Sargent, Judith Seltzer, Scott Slater, Fran Smith, The Seven Deuces, Tom and Anne Snyder, Jesse Solomon, Terrence Tivnan, Susan Wadsworth, Jason Walker, Nancy Walser, Janie Ward, Brady and Cora Weissbourd, Margot Welch, and Min Zhou.

I owe this book to the scores of people who volunteered to be formally interviewed or more informally took up my questions about how to raise moral children.

My children, Jake, David, and Sophie, learned to spot me winding up to ask them a book-related question from a mile away. They rolled their eyes and skewered me mercilessly, but they never stopped engaging my questions and refused to let me sink into clichés about children.

God knows, enough has been written about the agonies of writing a book, but perhaps not enough about the pleasure. Yet there was a pure and deep pleasure in writing this book—the deep pleasure of talking to my wife about what it means to be a moral parent. She did everything humanly possible to support and improve this book: she pored over countless drafts, shared her great insights, told me gently when my writing was boring or my ideas dumb. She also models every day the quality that I think is at the center of morality—the capacity to take other perspectives and to make the needs of others as real and compelling as one's own. This book unspools from our life together and it is for her every step of the way.

This book is dedicated to my parents. It has deep roots in their parenting and their work. They devoted much of their lives to understanding children's development and to strengthening families, and they taught me, among many things, about the wonder and energy of asking moral questions and constructing with others a moral understanding of the world.

While the stories described herein are true, names and other details have been changed to ensure confidentiality. In several instances, to protect individuals' privacy and to sharpen meanings,
I created composite portraits. A few times, I've described my experiences or the experiences of a family member, and used pseud-
onyms and changed identifying details.

The research reflected in this book was conducted in part in
three high schools in the Boston area—an independent school
with a largely affluent population in a town near Boston, a high-
poverty Boston public school, and an ethnically and economically
diverse public school just outside of Boston—as well as in two
small-town high schools in the South. At each of these schools, we
surveyed about forty students, primarily juniors. We conducted
face-to-face interviews with students and parents in the three Boston-area high schools and in one of the southern schools to understand more deeply the meaning of and context for students' survey
responses, and to further explore ideas and issues raised in the survey. The surveys and interviews primarily tried to elicit from students their moral questions and dilemmas, their sense of how their
parents were promoting their morality, how they weighed—and
how they imagined their parents weighed—their goodness in relation to other aspirations such as happiness and achievement, their
perception of racial differences in social and moral challenges and
qualities, and the nature and degree of their idealism.

We also conducted five focus groups with students across the
three Boston-area schools. In the early stages of the research,
knowing the limitations of what children will discuss with adults,
I enlisted two high school students in one school who consulted
with me on the development of the survey and who interviewed
about a dozen other students over the course of the year.

This book is also based on interviews and more informal conversations with parents—as well as informal observations of fam-

ilies—in many parts of the country, including Chicago, Washington, D.C., San Francisco, and New York. I also talked to numerous teachers, sports coaches, mental health professionals, and other professionals involved in children's lives. I lived this book for many years and found myself discussing the issues it raises in many different kinds of contacts with people in many different settings. Finally, I have drawn on several occasions from research I conducted in the late 1980s and 1990s on children and families for a project on childhood vulnerability.

While we were thus able to collect a good deal of information about how children and adults think about morality across a wide array of ethnicities, economic classes, and geographical areas, the interviews and survey responses in this book are clearly not representative of the diversity of families in the United States. My findings here are intended to be only suggestive, and my hope is that they will prompt more questions, more research, and more reflection about the moral lives of American families.

THE PARENTS WE MEAN TO BE

For many years, as a psychologist and a parent, I have kept my ear tuned to the latest wisdom parents receive about how to raise children who will become caring, strong, and responsible people. I have combed popular articles, tracked politicians' ideas, gathered advice from talk show experts.

The basic messages are predictable: single parenthood, peer pressure, and popular culture are destroying our children's moral foundations. Parents and other adults are failing as role models and neglecting to teach children basic moral values and standards. Kids need to know right from wrong. According to a major survey by the organization Public Agenda, more than six in ten American adults identified "as a very serious problem" young people's failure to learn fundamental moral values, including honesty, respect, and responsibility for others.

There is, to be sure, some truth in these explanations for children's moral troubles. I have seen the powerful influence of peer pressure on my own kids, and my wife and I certainly try to limit their exposure to aspects of popular culture that seem designed to obliterate every particle of their humanity. Children need constructive role models who teach right from wrong.

But for anyone who is willing to enter children's worlds and look hard at what shapes their development, there is much about these explanations that is mystifying, if not deeply unsettling. At best they miss the point; at worst they are a kind of massive cover-up and cop-out. Blaming peers and popular culture lets adults off the hook—and dangerously so. It dodges a fundamental truth that is supported by a mountain of research. Children's moral development is decided by many factors, including not only media and peer influences but their genetic endowment, birth order, gender, and how these different factors interact. Yet *we* are the primary influence on children's moral lives. The parent-child relationship is at the center of the development of all the most important moral qualities, including honesty, kindness, loyalty, generosity, a commitment to justice, the capacity to think through moral dilemmas, and the ability to sacrifice for important principles.

While there's nothing wrong with exhorting adults to be better role models and to teach values, this by itself does nothing to help people actually be and do these things. I don't know any adult who became a better role model simply by being told to be one. Nor do these exhortations reach the heart of what it is to be a person who is an effective parent, a true moral mentor.

What I am acutely aware matters most as a parent is not whether my wife and I are "perfect" role models or how much we talk about values, but the hundreds of ways — as living, breathing, imperfect human beings — we influence our children in the complex, messy relationships we have with them day to day.

This knowledge came to me gradually in the first years of my children's lives, but there was one specific afternoon when it struck me most sharply. Sunday afternoons were sacrosanct, reserved for family outings. My three kids are three years apart, and it was often hard to find something that was fun for everyone.

One blustery, sunny Sunday, we went to a park near the ocean. My oldest son, then about seven years old, was withdrawn and seemed listless. The park was not his favorite place. My week had been stressful, and I'd been looking forward to this outing. I lashed out at him for sulking. We had done what he'd wanted to do the Sunday before, I reminded him, and I expected him to rally, to cheerfully participate. It also seemed to me that this was an opportunity to reinforce a basic notion of reciprocity.

My wife certainly agreed with me that our son should be expected to engage in activities for the sake of the family. But, she pointed out, he seemed more tired than unhappy, and she reminded me that I, too, could seem less than enthusiastic during family activities I didn't enjoy. She added, gently, that perhaps I should rethink whether the real issue in this case was teaching my son a moral standard. Instead, maybe I'd gotten angry because I'd been expecting this family event to pull me out of my own bad mood.

After some grumbling, I came to see that my wife was right. I apologized to my son and explained to him that I had had a rough week. But what dawned on me suddenly was that under the guise of teaching my son a principle, I had made it harder for him to care about how I thought or felt, more self-protective, and perhaps a little less willing to pitch in for the family. What also hit me was that while this single event wouldn't do lasting damage, many times a week we had interactions with our kids in which my wife and I succeeded—or failed—in disentangling and balancing our needs and theirs and in enabling them to take other perspectives, and that these interactions, cumulatively, defined their notion of what a relationship is and powerfully shaped their capacity for caring, respectful relationships. Our children's moral qualities were also shaped day to day by what we registered, or failed to acknowledge, in the world around us, and what we asked them to register—whether we let them treat a store clerk as invisible, or commented when a child in a playground had been treated un fairly, or pointed out to them a neighbor's good deed. We were, too, constantly affecting their moral abilities by how we defined their responsibilities for others, and by whether we insisted that those responsibilities be met. Our effectiveness as moral mentors has hinged, most basically, on whether we have earned our children's respect and trust by, among many things, admitting our errors and explaining our decisions to them in ways that they see as fair. It was these day-to-day details of our relationship with our children—far more than our talk about values—that formed their moral core.

What has clearly been hardest for my wife and me—and for every parent we know—is being vigilant about these things when we have been stressed or depleted or outright depressed. There are "strategies" that can help us with our children during these critical moments, to be sure. But what is fundamentally being challenged at these times are our moral qualities and maturity—including our ability to manage our flaws—qualities that can't be feigned. The reason many children in this country continually lack vital moral qualities is that we have failed to come to grips with the fundamental reality that we bring our *selves* to the project of raising a moral child. That makes being a parent or mentor a profound moral test, and learning to raise children well a profound moral achievement.

This book offers, then, a very different view of moral development than the ideas currently dominating the airwaves. It is a view gleaned over the past several years from my own experiences as a parent, from informal conversations with parents, observations of families, from interviews that I, along with my research team, have conducted with scores of children and adults—parents, teachers, sports coaches—as well as from a survey of about 200 children.

Much of what we found was heartening. Many parents care deeply about their children's moral qualities, and we uncovered a wide variety of effective parenting practices across race, ethnicity, and class. This book takes up key, illuminating variations in these practices.

Yet we also found much that is troubling. Some adults hold misguided beliefs about raising moral children, and some parents have little investment in their children's character. And the bigger problem is more subtle: a wide array of parents and other adults are unintentionally—in largely unconscious ways—undermining the development of critical moral qualities in children.

This book reveals this largely hidden psychological landscape—the unexamined ways that parents, teachers, sports coaches, and other mentors truly shape moral and emotional development. It explores, for example, the subtle ways that adults can put their own happiness first or put their children's happiness above all else, imperiling both children's ability to care about others and, ironically, their happiness. It shows not only how achievement-obsessed parents can damage children, but also how many of us as parents have unacknowledged fears about our children's achievements that can erode our influence as moral mentors and diminish children's capacity to invest in others. It explores why a positive parent instinct that is suddenly widespread—the desire to be closer to children—can have great moral benefits to children in certain circumstances but can cause parents to confuse their needs with children's, jeopardizing children's moral growth. It reveals how the most intense, invested parents can end up subtly shaming their children and eroding their moral qualities, and it shows the hidden ways that parents and college mentors can undermine young people's idealism.

At the same time, this book describes inspiring parents, teachers, and coaches who avoid these pitfalls, as well as concrete strategies for raising moral and happy children. And it makes the case that parents and other adults have great potential for moral growth. Moral development is a lifelong project. Parenting can either cause us to regress or cultivate in us new, powerful capacities for caring, fairness, and idealism, with large consequences for our children. What is often exciting about parenting is not only the unveiling of our children's moral and emotional capacities, but the unveiling of our own.

Finally, this book seeks to shift attention away from our heavy focus on teaching values, toward other, more effective approaches. One problem with the values approach becomes instantly clear when talking to children as young as six years old: the great majority of children are quite articulate about values and standards and many see as patronizing the perception that they lack them. Research reveals that even children as young as three and four years old often know that stealing is wrong, even without being explicitly told by adults.

That's not to say—and this can't be shouted loudly enough—that children do not have a problem with values. But the problem is different: it is actually *living* by values, such as fairness, caring, and responsibility, day to day. Sixteen-year-old Bill Heron knows that he laughed too hard and too long when a friend put a fart machine under the desk of a new girl in class, but he didn't want to "spoil the joke" for everyone. Fourteen-year-old Sarah Hamlin knows that she should reach out to a new kid at school, but she "gets too busy." Ten-year-old Juan Maltez knows that teasing can be hurtful, but he believes that if he stops teasing, he'll be tagged a loser: "I'll slide right into the sea of dorks." As a quite direct sixteen-year-old said to me: "I'm taking this class where they're trying to help us figure out how to determine what's right from wrong. But the kids at my school all know right from wrong. That's not the problem. The problem is that some kids just don't give a shit."

These children don't need us to define the goal. That's easy. The challenges for us are much harder and deeper. One of them is to help children deal with the emotions, such as the fear of being a pariah or a "loser," that cause them to transgress. Emotions are often the runaway bus; values, the driver desperately gripping the wheel.

A second critical challenge is to help children develop a deep, abiding commitment to these values, a commitment that can override other needs and goals. The issue isn't moral literacy; it's moral motivation. There is one capacity in particular that is at the heart of such motivation—appreciation, the capacity to know and value others, including those different in background and perspective. Appreciation brakes destructive impulses—there is no more powerful deterrent to lying, stealing, or tormenting those who are different—and inspires caring, responsibility, and generosity. This book will provide a kind of map for parents for developing in children this vital quality.

A third challenge is to develop in children a strong sense of self—so that they can withstand adversity in the service of moral goals—and to ingrain in children from early ages the habits of attending to and caring for others. The self-sacrificing acts of Europeans who rescued Jews from the Nazis in World War II, research by Samuel and Pearl Oliner suggests, were not matters of deliberation. They were acts that emerged from these individuals' basic self-concepts and dispositions. As one rescuer puts it: "I insist on saying that it was absolutely natural to have done this [rescuing]. You don't have to glorify yourself—considering that we are all children of God and that it is impossible to distinguish between one human and another." It is possible to weave values such as responsibility into children's sense of self from an early age, to make caring for others as reflexive as breathing.

In all these ways, then, this book seeks to generate a new conversation about how to raise moral children. Especially as children become adolescents, it may seem impossible to shield them from crass media images or the strong pull of morally mindless peer groups. Yet in the end, if we are determined, self-reflective, and open to counsel from our loved ones, we can both create in our children a strong moral core early in childhood and be strong guides for them in navigating the troubles of adolescence and young adulthood. This book is about how.

What are the real sources of our children's morality? How, concretely, can we develop appreciation in children and shape the critical emotions underlying morality? How can we cultivate our own moral and mentoring abilities and better direct the many hidden currents that are shaping our children's moral and emotional lives?

1

HELPING CHILDREN MANAGE
DESTRUCTIVE EMOTIONS

A FEW YEARS AGO I was playing pickup basketball at a YMCA in Chicago with a friend, Jack, a wiry, gracious younger man. Pickup basketball provides all sorts of opportunities to shine or regress morally. It is sometimes difficult in these games to distinguish, in fact, disturbed behavior from normal forms of male competitive idiocy. This day, it dawned on me slowly that a young man we were playing against, Phil, whom we had just met, was playing in a kind of steady fever of unfocused rage. He wasn't trash-talking—that controlled, refined, intelligent art—he was simply dumbly insulting other players, including his own teammates: "You suck," "You have no game." When other players called fouls on him or complained about his flying elbows and other stretching-the-rules assaults, he became theatrically aggrieved. Phil and Jack were covering each other, and the elbowing and insulting were bringing Jack close to some kind of breaking point. Yet Jack managed to stay fairly even-keeled, telling Phil to "calm down" or to "just play the game."

Several months later, though, Jack and Phil again encountered each other in a game, and this time things did not go smoothly. Phil was once again ripping his teammates and disrespecting opponents' calls, and Jack, his competitive juices roiling, vowed to step up his game, to give Phil a harsh lesson in humility. Almost instantly, taunts were exchanged. Jack then drove to the basket and was clotheslined by Phil—Phil hit him hard with his shoulder in the upper body, driving Jack to the floor. Jack popped up, yelling epithets. The response was swift and unequivocal. Phil lofted a huge wad of spit that spattered across Jack's face.

Jack found himself in a hated, almost forgotten childhood state: "I hadn't been in a fight since I was a teenager, and here I was throwing haymakers, roundhouse punches at this guy, and missing everything." Other players quickly intervened, pulling Jack and Phil apart. Phil was utterly unrepentant. Jack quickly picked up his sports bag and walked off the court.

Jack was apoplectic. "I couldn't believe that I had actually been drawn into a fight. More than anything, I was embarrassed. I had recently been elected a member of the local Chamber of Commerce, and there I was taking swings at this guy. And there was another reason I was furious at myself. As much as I love and admire my father, he was always doing crazy stuff like getting into fights when I was growing up, which was embarrassing for me. And I really didn't want to be like that at a time when I was trying to build my career as an upstanding young lawyer. The fight was like a bad sign that I hadn't been able to fall as far from the tree as I had hoped."

Jack couldn't let the episode go. He went to the front desk of the YMCA and asserted that both he and Phil should be suspended. He then wrote a letter to the president of the Y, apologizing and again suggesting the suspension, arguing that "our level of stupidity" should not be tolerated and that "consistency and zero tolerance should be the hallmark of the Y's policy on fighting of any sort." The president called the next day to say that Phil's membership was being terminated—there had been many complaints about Phil—and, for consistency, Jack's membership was being suspended for three months.

Almost all great literature concerns moral questions, for morality cannot be extracted from that which moves us, from our emotions. The emotions are at the root of our moral beliefs and be-havior. While positive emotions such as empathy, admiration, and affection propel our caring and generosity, certain painful emo-tions are vital to our morality as well. Emotions such as shame, guilt, and fear protect us as a society—to avoid shame and guilt, we follow moral standards and rules, refrain from aggression, cru-elty, arrogance, greed. These emotions are also the engines of moral learning: they can generate more refined and complex moral beliefs. Jack's shame and guilt over fighting pushed him to sort out what was central to his integrity and how he might act to support his best moral instincts. Because moderate amounts of these painful emotions are constructive in these ways, it's perilous when adults seek to erase them from children's lives.

Yet when children or adults have to deal with heavy doses of these feelings, and when they lack constructive strategies for man-aging them, negative emotions can be a constant, destructive un-dertow, sometimes swamping moral impulses and convictions. Harvard child psychologist Jerome Kagan observes that the reason violence-prevention programs that explain to children the harm-ful consequences of violence don't help "is because children know violence is wrong—what they can't control is the shame and de-structive impulses that fuel violence." The problem with Jack is not that he lacks values or appreciation—Jack has great integrity and humanity. The problem is that he finds himself suddenly flooded with humiliation and anger (and he has a clear image from his father about how to respond).

When children or adults like Phil are in an almost constant state of self-righteous rage—hunting opportunity to belittle others—shame is often a core, hounding aspect of the self. Their rage masks their self-doubts and protects them from almost literally drown-ing in shame. When Bill, the sixteen-year-old mentioned in the introduction, plays along with the cruel fart-machine gag, he succumbs to a need for recognition and approval. When thirteen-year-old Matt steals from his friends' homes because, as he ex-plains, he can't bear it that other kids have more money than he does, envy and a sense of inferiority are at work. When, to avoid being snitches, children lie to teachers about whether there will be a fight after school, anxiety about being ostracized compels them.

Further, when negative feelings are constant and excessive, children are apt to develop primitive moral beliefs. Cheating, driven by fears of failure and inferiority, has become so common and ingrained in many schools—in one survey almost 75 percent of high school students admit to cheating—that children we interviewed have developed all sorts of ways of justifying it: "It's worth it to get into a good college"; "If the person knows you're cheating from them, what's the big deal?"; and the classic bailout: "Everybody does it." Some children will justify stealing because "society is corrupt" or because "people really only care about themselves." Some children develop entire moral systems that help them manage their feelings of shame and inferiority. The intricate moral code of some gangs, for instance, rationalizes death as the punishment for disrespect.

While many different emotions can shape children's moral development, there are two painful emotions that are especially troubling: shame, an acute feeling of unworthiness and embarrassment, and the fear of disapproval and isolation. While these emotions at normal levels are vital, large numbers of children are dealing with high levels of shame and intense fear of disapproval, and these levels can lead to all sorts of transgressions in both children and adults. And the irony is that as more and more parents are obsessed with their children's happiness and are working hard to protect their children's positive emotional states, they are unknowingly fueling precisely these two negative emotions.

How are we as parents and mentors stoking these feelings, and how can we stop? When children suffer high levels of shame and fear of disapproval, how can we help them manage these feelings?

First, shame.

SHAME AND INFERIORITY

For twenty-five years, the psychiatrist and researcher James Gilligan worked with prison inmates who had committed serious, often grotesque violent crimes. While these crimes had many sources, Gilligan uncovered one common denominator: "I have yet to see a serious act of violence that was not provoked by the experience of feeling shamed and humiliated." These criminals, Gilligan observed, had typically "lived for a lifetime on a diet of contempt and disdain." The risk of shame became for them worse than the risk of death. "The most dangerous men on earth," Gilligan says, "are those who are afraid that they are wimps."

There may be no feelings more responsible for destruction than shame and inferiority. One reels at the number of wars and genocides ignited by some real or imagined indignity—Hitler was quite explicit about seeking to wipe out the humiliation of Germany in World War I, the "shame of Versailles." Yet the violations caused by shame and a sense of inferiority are mostly prosaic and everyday. When a teenager cheats on a test because she is terrified of not being accepted into a prestigious college, lies to her friends about her father's job because she perceives his occupation as lowly, or seeds a rumor about another child whom she perceives as undercutting her popularity, shame and a sense of inferiority typically lurk at the root. Much has been made about the pervasiveness in our country of narcissism—a troubling brew of arrogance, a sense of entitlement, and an inability to empathize—and psychologists have long recognized that narcissism is rooted in early experiences of humiliation. The damage done by shaming, as Hitler's terrible vengeance reveals, also often spreads, viruslike. Shamed adults often teach others how they feel—Phil spits on Jack—and children who are shamed are likely to shame other children, and eventually their own children. Some of our greatest plays—take Eugene O'Neill's *Long Day's Journey into Night*—are about family mem-

bers, riven with shame, who can't stop needling each other's defects and unburying each other's humiliations, while withholding
precisely the kinds of reassurance and love that remove shame's
deep sting.

The reason shame is so dangerous becomes clear when it is
compared with its cousin, guilt. Guilt is the self-reproach we experience when we violate an inner standard—when we cheat on a
spouse, undercut a colleague, fail to report a crime. When guilt is
serious, as in Jack's case, we feel the need to atone; until the wrong
is set right the world can feel on hold and out of joint. A path to
correct this state usually presents itself—guilt insists on and often
reveals solutions.

Shame, in these respects, is not so easy. As shame scholar Robert
Karen notes, one is usually not ashamed about a deed, about what
one has *done,* but about who one *is,* and especially by the perception that our defects have been exposed and are seen by a real or
imagined audience. As the legendary psychiatrist Helen Block
Lewis put it: "We say I am ashamed of *myself.* [But that] I am guilty
for something." Shame and guilt, as in Jack's case, are often entan-
gled, and one way people may alleviate shame is by converting it
into guilt. In writing the note to the YMCA president, Jack may
unconsciously be acting to repair both the guilt of breaking a law
and of violating another person and the shame of doing so quite
publicly. But because it is so often hard to convert or repair shame,
it often festers inside the self. When shame accumulates, or when
it has been stamped into the self at an early age—and when people
have limited strategies for dealing with it—the chances of it corroding appreciation and moral motivation and expressing itself
destructively are unnervingly high.

Children may, of course, suffer many kinds of shame for many
reasons. The landscape of some children's lives from early ages is
shaped by the possibility of shame, because of a disability, say, or
because of frequent contact with race, ethnic, or class stereotypes.
But it is we as parents who play the primary role in protecting chil-

dren from shame—author and child advocate Marian Wright Edelman describes, for example, how important her parents and other community adults were in counteracting the barrage of racist messages she endured growing up as a black girl in the Deep South—and, distressingly, it is we as parents who can create in children the deepest and most lasting forms of shame. We may indirectly set our children up for shame, as Karen observes, if we don't teach them manners, or if we inflate their importance, or fail to see or curb their obnoxious traits. When parents give children too much autonomy—when they give children's impulses too much rein or when they give children too much power to make choices they are not prepared to make—they can set children up for shame as well.

But we will never get far in alleviating shame if we can't stop ourselves from doing the more direct things we do to create it, and if we can't reduce certain troubling and pervasive modern forms of shaming. For many years, as a therapist, I was most concerned about a particular kind of direct shaming, as were many of my colleagues. One of my patients, a forty-year-old man whom I will call Sam, returned again and again to a time, when he was eleven years old, when his mother purposely hung bed sheets he had wet out to dry on the front lawn, in plain view of neighborhood children. Even thirty years later, the memory produced in him a terrible anger—he described it as a stampede in his head—and was a kind of hole that drained any empathy he had for his mother, even as she aged and became infirm. It's a kind of chestnut in child development that the even more destructive parents are those who express to children that they are ashamed of *them*, who criticize not just a behavior, but some core, self-defining, immutable trait—that their child is not pretty enough, or smart enough, or as nice as another child down the block. An eighty-year-old friend can still feel searing shame when she remembers her father telling her when she turned eighteen that it was the first time, because she could not be drafted, that he was happy that she was a girl and not a boy.

There's no question that this kind of shaming can be terribly harmful to children. Because we never forget our humiliations, because shame has a terrible capacity to stay fresh, shame can constantly tear at our capacity to respect or forgive those who may in other ways have cared diligently for us—consider my patient Sam and his mother. When this shaming is chronic, it can create a core, lasting feeling of defect or wrongness and amass angers that constantly compromise one's capacity for empathy and appreciation—consider the prisoners interviewed by Gilligan. And this kind of direct shaming is common in certain communities. Some athletic coaches are quite explicit about using insults and slights to awaken the fiercest forms of desire in children, for instance.

But as much as we fret about this kind of shaming, there is evidence, at least in middle-class communities, that it has greatly waned. A study by psychologist Peggy Miller and her colleagues suggests that middle-class American mothers, concerned about children's self-esteem, strongly condemn shaming children. In a culture such as ours that is so attuned to every kind of emotional vulnerability, including shame—in the last thirty years there may have been more psychological talk in our country than in any country in the history of humankind—shaming has itself become stigmatized. Because shame is so agonizing and vivid, it is an easy target for the growing ranks of experts who now police our emotional lives. Racks of books alert parents to the ravages of shaming; self-help gurus like John Bradshaw have barnstormed around the country, imploring parents to stop humiliating their kids; and legions of psychotherapists and airwave experts raise up the evils of deriding kids' traits or embarrassing them in front of others.

Yet that leaves a large puzzle. For while overt shaming has been on the decline, there appears to be no comparable decrease in the number of children or young adults who are dealing with serious shame. Many psychologists are now claiming that shame is pervasive; some are saying, in fact, that it's more pervasive than ever before. And our culture seems obsessed with shame. Several popular television shows—*American Idol,* and MTV's *Room Raiders* and *Punk'd*—gorge on humiliation, and feed, almost pornographically, on the overexposure of our most private self-doubts. These shows may unconsciously rivet so many Americans because they create tension around the constant threat of humiliation—they play on our fears of shame.

That shame continues to be so prevalent results, to be sure, from complex social forces—including the staggering numbers of children abandoned by fathers, our increased focus on our selves as opposed to our communities, and our growing obsession with high-profile achievement (topics I take up in later chapters). But it results, too, from the fact that parents can shame their children in many ways, and often in ways neither they nor their children are even aware of. (The good news, as I take up later, is that there is much we can do about these current forms of shaming.)

Take nineteen-year-old Jim Starans, growing up in an affluent community on Long Island. From an early age, he recalls, he lived with a strange kind of dissonance. His parents repeatedly told him that he had it all. And indeed it seemed to him that he had every thing. He had every possible material comfort. He went to highly respected schools and lived in a community of people he respected. Jim was the last child from his mom's second marriage, and she told him that she had "perfected" her parenting by the time she got to him. Jim admitted that it was hard to remember a time when his mother or stepfather—a man he described as kind and gentle although somewhat remote—spoke to him harshly.

Still, Jim struggled almost constantly with shameful self-doubts. He would feel that he was "caving in" with shame when he didn't make the honor roll at his school, and almost any form of slight could cut to the bone, throwing him into a tailspin of self-doubt. At times he was hard on himself for being an ingrate—he should feel better, he told himself, given how lucky he was. He tried to talk to his mother about these feelings, and sometimes he found her very tuned in to him and empathic. Yet she could also be dismissive. He remembers learning in a high school human development class about low self-esteem, and reporting to his mother that he thought he had it. She snapped back, "That's ridiculous." Often he found himself irritated and angry at her, and getting into petty fights with her, without really knowing why.

While Jim was never a victim of direct shaming, he grew up in a family environment that makes shame almost inevitable. When parents define happiness narrowly and rigidly and satiate children's every need in terms of it—when they define happiness in terms of material satisfaction or attending good schools, for example, as Jim's parents do, and then make a big show of gratifying these needs—they can set children up for shame. Many kinds of neediness, disappointment, or uncertainty can make these children feel that there is something wrong with them.

Children can similarly come to believe that the only explanation for their troubles is their own defects when their families are idealized by their parents or when their parents fail to surface their own flaws—as Jim's mother does when she suggests that Jim should be happy because her own parenting has been "perfect." In a world presented like this, any child can feel like an ungrateful worm when they suffer many kinds of misery. Further, when parents become too focused on a measure of a child's worth—whether high-status achievement or popularity or attractiveness—children can clearly feel shame when they sense that they aren't passing the spoken or unspoken tests.

Perhaps the most common and damaging kind of shame, though, is when parents are threatened by their children's feelings and weaknesses. A bald example is Jim's mom recoiling from the notion that he has low self-esteem, but many parents have difficulty tolerating their children's flaws and troubling feelings—anxieties, angers, disappointments, even sadness. One sees parents on playgrounds, disturbed by any sign of anxiety or letdown in their child, leap up to try to "fix" it. There are clearly panicked parents these days who rush their children to therapists at the first stirring of trouble. As a parent who heads a school parent council recently said to me, "What I hear from teachers is that lots of parents want their kids to be perfect and they can't bear hearing about any problem or weakness." Yet if an idealized parent, the person a child wants to grow up to be, can't deal with a feeling or flaw, then a child may experience these feelings or flaws as wrong, as defects in the self. Feelings such as anger, jealousy, and even shame itself can become sources of shame. And "nothing is more shameful than to feel ashamed," as James Gilligan puts it.

Parents may be threatened by their children's negative feelings and weaknesses for many reasons. Some parents are swamped with guilt over neglecting their children. Often children's negative feelings resonate with parents' own unresolved, troubling feelings or are dissonant with what parents expect their child to be or of how they expect their family to function—consider again Jim and his mother. The book and film *Ordinary People* is a classic study of a mother who recoils from and is enraged by her son's agonies because they violate her postcard image of her family. What makes matters worse is that these threatened parents may go to great lengths to whitewash children's problems to the outside world, only inflating the shame children attach to their negative feelings. Research indicates that affluent families especially are more likely to keep troubles private—in some cases it is excessive attention to how they are perceived that has driven the quest for wealth in the first place—and that many affluent families are concerned about maintaining a veneer of well-being because they believe that they should be better able to deal with problems than those less fortunate. Affluent families may also feel that they should have fewer problems in the first place.

But the irony is that for a large number of parents, like Jim's mom, this failure may be the downside of an overall positive trend. What I hear from both teachers and parents these days is that parents who bridle at even the slightest criticism of their parenting are often not neglectful at all. In fact, they are parents who are heavily involved with their children, sometimes micromanaging their children's lives. While many children have less access to parents these days than forty years ago because more mothers are working and more fathers have vanished, middle-class children today spend more time with parents during leisure time than children at almost any other time in history. These parents, like Jim's mom, often feel that they are doing everything for their children and are having a direct and large impact on their emotional lives. And precisely because they are doing so much—because a great deal of their self-esteem is wrapped up in parenting—the stakes of failing as a parent are very high. For some of these parents, any sign of parenting failure, any expression of distress, anger, doubt, or weakness in a child, is an attack on their fundamental sense of competence.

And the troubling fact is that many parents are still expressing contempt for their children, they are just doing it in ways, again, that neither they nor their children are quite conscious of. In videotaping mothers' interactions with their children, professor and pediatric researcher Michael Lewis observed that mothers in middle-class communities were quite careful both to avoid verbally expressing contempt for their children and to focus on children's behavior and not their traits. But Lewis found that many mothers, in criticizing their children's behavior, were also exhibiting disgust in their facial expressions. Karen quotes Lewis: "We're finding that 30–40 percent of mothers' prohibitions are accompanied by [these elements of disgust]. And this is in laboratory situations, where they know they're being videotaped . . . We think we have moved to a higher plane because we don't punish the kids, when in fact we may be humiliating them instead." This disgust, Lewis writes, is "all the more effective because it is secretive. The disgusted face is made very quickly, and parents can deny that they made it; or, if they admit to it, they can deny it was detected by the child." Because so many of us lead pressure-cooker lives and are stressed and exhausted, we also at times need immediate compliance from our children, and there's no question that shaming children, powerful as it is, can get fast results.

Just as distressing, we at times may be letting others do the shaming for us. We might, for example, give far too much rein, often half-consciously, to the "special forces" of humiliation—siblings—with their hawklike skills at spotting and boring in on every kind of imperfection. We might never comment about a child being overweight, say, yet we do little to block a sibling's barrage of fat jokes. Sometimes parents fail to protect their children from the humiliations of peers, or even collude with these peers in hidden ways.

This is a fraught, troubling realm. Hard as it is to recover or heal when one has been exposed to shaming that is vivid and direct, it can be trickier still for children to recover from shaming that they are not conscious of, or when they may not even know who the real perpetrator is. Children like Jim have a harder time fighting back or developing coping capacities or pointing out to a parent what is harming them, so even parents who are working hard to become better parents may not get any feedback. Children may find themselves angry at their parents, but without any reason they can put their finger on. They wind up ashamed of this anger as well. Parent-child relationships can sour; fights spring up, as they do with Jim and his mom, over little things and the wrong things. Children not only live with destructive levels of shame, but parents' moral authority is eroded.

The goal, of course, is not to go back to openly shaming our children. The reduction in overt, intentional shaming is important progress. What makes explicit shaming so troubling is that effective parents, teachers, or coaches *never* need to intentionally shame their children. When children respect us, our moral standards and expectations and limit-setting will both be effective and induce some shame, and that is altogether healthy and natural. A child will feel some shame, for example, when he or she is removed from a room for hitting another child. We certainly should not refrain from setting standards or walk on eggshells because our children might feel shame. We can, instead, commit to setting clear expectations and to using positive reinforcement in order to reduce unnecessary punishments.

The goal should be to build on the progress we have made: we as parents can do a great deal to avoid unnecessarily shaming our children. We can better police siblings who are bent on humiliation, and adhere to a few straightforward guidelines. Whenever possible, we should reprimand or discipline children privately—punishing or embarassing children in front of others can easily overwhelm them with shame—and we can pick up warning signs that our children feel too much shame, such as high sensitivity to slights or insults of any kind. This sensitivity should inform our discipline strategies—sometimes simply raising our voice, for instance, can induce significant shame. We can, too, work to pause and take a reflective stance when our children are struggling with difficult feelings. Rather than seeking to solve the problem immediately, we can start by being curious and collecting information. Jim's mom might have asked him, for example, why he thought he had "low self-esteem." She might have wondered aloud with him what kinds of things had happened to make him feel down on himself, and she might have brainstormed with him about what might make him feel better.

We can also consciously avoid idealizing or marketing our parenting or our family to our children. That doesn't mean we shouldn't point out occasionally aspects of our parenting and our families that our children should appreciate. But, in general, it's important to enable our children to come to their own understandings of our parenting and their family's strengths and weaknesses.

At the same time, we can seek to hold in our heads a complex message about child development. Many parents feel ashamed of themselves or they are threatened by their children's feelings, as seems to be the case with Jim's mom, because they see their children's problems as directly resulting from their own parenting flaws. Yet while the point of this book is to discern the many powerful ways adults shape children's moral development, it is equally critical to disabuse adults of the myth that there is a simple, linear relationship between their parenting and their child's troubles. It's not as if parenting behavior X always leads to child behavior Y. Strong research has overturned the traditional psychodynamic model that places almost all childhood woes at the door of parenting defects—a model that for decades shamed parents for even serious childhood diseases, such as schizophrenia and autism, that are now known to have clear biological roots. The role of temperament and biology in children's development, we now know, is profound. Parents need a model in their heads of children's development that reflects the major role of parenting but that also takes into account the interaction of parenting, biology, family functioning, peers, and other factors in creating their children's strengths and vulnerabilities.

When it comes to preventing ourselves from shaming children, what will be most important, though, is self-awareness. To develop that self-awareness may require, in part, having the courage to ask our spouses or close friends and relatives to give us occasional feedback about our parenting practices—a topic I take up in the final chapter. That may be the only way that some parents can become aware that they are using disgust, for instance, to motivate and manage their children.

Hard as it can be, it's also critical for us to pay attention to our own negative feelings about our children, and to recognize how our own fear and shame can cause us to shame our children. Most of us have moments at least when we recognize that we are threatened by our children's feelings or are ashamed of our children. While we tend to make a hard and fast distinction between conscious and unconscious thoughts and feelings, most unconscious thoughts are not entirely repressed—they occasionally flutter into our consciousness. And these thoughts and feelings are usually altogether natural. They come with being a parent.

Yet because of the damage these feelings can do when they are deep and chronic, it's vital that we get to the bottom of them, for often at their root is some unhealthy attitude or feeling that we haven't dealt with effectively—our attempts to hold on to a notion of happiness that may no longer even work for us, our worry about our own capacities as a parent, our wish that a child conform to an image of success that doesn't make sense for him or her, our thwarted ambitions, our own hectoring, unresolved shame. For some parents who are struggling with serious shame, feeling proud of their child is always an uphill battle—after all, how can they, unworthy and defective as they are, have a child who is *not* unworthy and defective? Whether we feel ashamed of ourselves and our children depends a great deal, too, on our emotional state. Depression can, for example, cause parents to fasten on their children's flaws. One study indicates that the longer fathers are unemployed, the more likely they are to describe their children negatively.

A modicum of self-awareness can go a long way. Depression researcher and child psychiatrist William Beardslee observes that self-awareness and self-understanding are critical in helping depressed parents manage their negative feelings and develop closer relationships with their children. Some self-understanding can also help us deal with many types of situations where we are vulnerable to feeling ashamed of our child. One parent told me, for example, that her mother criticized her son for being lazy and that her first instinct was to turn around and be angry at him. But rather than lashing out, she was able to see that she was too sensitive to this kind of disapproval from her mother. She decided to postpone talking to her son about this issue until she had more "data" about whether his supposed laziness was, in fact, a pattern.

And because shame so stunts our capacity for self-knowledge and growth and so impairs our relationships with our children, dealing with unintended shaming is not just a matter of our parenting effectiveness but of our well-being. When we have the capacity to see ourselves both clearly and generously—as people struggling with our own demons and weaknesses, who are prone to confuse our deficiencies with our children's—we can stop shaming our children and feel more of the self-empathy we need to feel gratification day to day. We will also be far more capable of the daily acts of authentic responsiveness that earn our children's lasting trust and love. Whenever we feel ashamed of our children, it should be a particular kind of red flag, a warning not to search out and inflate our children's flaws but to better understand our own.

FEAR OF DISAPPROVAL AND HELPING TEENS STAND UP FOR THEMSELVES

Early on a Saturday night, Lisa's boarding school roommate unexpectedly brought two friends, Katie and Monica, into their room, along with the makings for gin and tonics. Katie had paid someone outside a liquor store to buy the gin. Katie asked Lisa if she wanted a drink, and Lisa, knowing that drinking is strictly forbidden at her school, quickly declined. Later that evening the resident adviser in the girls' dorm found Monica reeking of liquor and vomiting violently in the bathroom. The adviser reported the incident to the school's disciplinary board.

The disciplinary board took immediate action, including asking Lisa and several other students in the dorm to appear before it. The board wanted to know both who was drinking and who had supplied the liquor.

Right up to the moment of the disciplinary hearing, Lisa was on the fence about whether to tell the truth. She knew the punishment for lying could be severe, but she also knew that if she told the truth, she could be consigned to social Siberia in her school. Katie was extremely popular.

While Lisa was waiting in the hall, the school's academic dean walked by and remarked sarcastically, not stopping to take in Lisa's response: "I hope you're proud of yourself." That seemed to turn a switch in Lisa. "It just made me feel like the adults in this school don't get it, that they don't deserve my respect."

At the hearing, Lisa was asked directly who bought the liquor. Lisa said she didn't know, but the board later uncovered from Monica that Katie had bragged to all the girls about how she had obtained the gin. The school was unforgiving: Lisa was expelled for her lie.

Lisa's father, a highly principled man, was furious at her. Lisa had been planning a ski trip over Christmas with her friends, but Lisa's father, as he put it, didn't want "to reward her" for failing to stand up for the truth, for being weak. Her mother, though, was worried that further punishing Lisa would alienate her from them. She didn't want to reward Lisa, but she also didn't want to jeopardize her connection to her daughter at a time when they were both reeling and when she worried that Lisa could spin dangerously out of her orbit. She decided to try to be "as supportive of Lisa as possible."

Lisa heard from her mother that her father wouldn't allow her to go on the ski trip, and went ballistic. "You guys say you want me to trust you," she told her mother, steel in her voice. "But I'll never tell Dad anything about my life, ever. You can make me come home, but I won't talk to him."

Again and again I hear parents fret that their children are dangerously hostage to their peers' approval—that they don't have a mind of their own or are incapable of standing up for what they believe. And there's no question that fear of disapproval and isolation, like shame, is responsible for many kinds of harm. It's not that peer groups are always, or even typically, destructive. There is a good deal of evidence, contrary to popular images, that peer groups can have many positive influences on children, including encouraging students to study hard and obtain good grades, to avoid smoking, and to be helpful to others. But acts of stupidity and cruelty generated by worshiping peer gods and goddesses are rampant, and the fear of disapproval and isolation can corrupt long into adulthood. Large numbers of adults collude with bigotry to avoid social stigma, violate principles rather than bear the ire of colleagues, or get caught in mob mentalities.

Whether children are able to tolerate disapproval and stay true to their moral beliefs and standards depends, among many factors, on whether they are temperamentally shy or assertive, on whether popularity is a mark of success in their families, and on how big a premium is placed on both self-assertion and tolerating disapproval in their families, cultures, or communities. Research also suggests that parents foster their children's ability to reason and act independently and to withstand disapproval when they respect their children's capacity to think from early ages and when they give their children input into key family decisions.

But this capacity to act independently depends primarily on the degree to which children have internalized moral values and on the strength of the self, the extent to which children can withstand adversity. Children need the self-sufficiency to be unbroken by periods of loneliness, and they need a stable enough self-image that their self-evaluations are more important than others' evaluations of them at any given moment.

But when children cross the border into adolescence, what many parents distressingly observe is not steady growth in the self and children's capacity to tolerate exclusion, but the seeming loss of the self. In many girls, especially, the capacity for self-assertion seems, in moral-development scholar Carol Gilligan's phrase, to "go underground." Making matters worse, most ways in which adults think to help children stand up for important principles tend to get no traction, and some backfire, as in the case of Lisa. Whether children as they become adults have a strong internal compass, then, depends not only on what children do or do not receive in early childhood but on how they emerge through adolescence.

The good news is that a great deal is known about how to help teenagers withstand disapproval and stand up for important principles. What gets in the way of adults facilitating this emergence? And what can adults do to help recapture and build in teenagers a stronger sense of self?

THE CONFLICTING MYTHS ABOUT TEENAGERS

Sometimes adults lose their effectiveness as mentors with teens — they become too angrily demanding — because of entirely understandable and even commendable worries. We may become harsh and exacting because we see adolescence as *the* critical period for shaping moral development, and because we naturally worry that our chances to influence our children's character are running out, that this may be our last opportunity to instill in children a strong moral core before they become adults. We are alarmed that our children might be dependent or selfish or spoiled forever.

Yet the struggles of teens to stand on important principles are fueled perhaps most commonly by two pervasive (and conflicting) adult myths. Rather than seeing teens' behavior as a function of a developmental stage — as we would the temper tantrum of a four-year-old — many of us, like Lisa's father, are distressed and angry because we mistakenly believe teens' capitulation to peers signals spinelessness, a lack of will. We view our teenagers as young adults who should be expected to take responsibility for their actions and to suffer consequences. Often parents and other adults indulge in "what's the matter with kids today?" discussions when teenagers fail to divulge to adults, say, that there is going to be a fight after school. In the film *West Side Story,* Officer Krupke famously drips with disdain for Riff and his gang, the Jets, because they won't tell him the location of a planned rumble between the

Jets and the Sharks. And when we see capitulation to peers as a sign of weakness, often our first instinct is that strong punishment can correct it or that children can be exhorted out of it. "We can't let our kids off the hook when they worry so much about snitching on their friends," is how one of our interviewees put it. "We need to tell our kids to be strong, that they have to stick up for what's right."

But as a good deal of psychological research has made clear for some time, important as it is for us as parents to stand for certain principles, when we dismiss or don't fully grasp children's fears of peer rejection, we are not really seeing who our children are — we are badly mistaking the basic nature of the adolescent self. Because for many adolescents, especially in early adolescence, the self derives its meaning largely from how it is known by peers. There is little outside this interpersonal self upon which to exert leverage or to hold one's ground, and so to risk peer rejection is not simply to endure a bout of loneliness. It is for many adolescents to feel, as psychologist and adolescence researcher Robert Kegan observes, that they "are losing the self itself." That's one reason Lisa is tied in knots about whether to snitch on her friends — the threat of losing the self, of staying in school and being friendless, is as threatening as the risk of expulsion, shameful as that is. And it's likely that Lisa cannot brook her father's anger because she feels, consciously or unconsciously, that he has no understanding of what is at her core and that she is being harshly punished for something that she experiences as outside her control. Lisa's father is driving her away at precisely that time when a strong connection to him, identification with his values, and access to his wisdom are exactly what she needs to develop greater moral independence.

The school's punishment of Lisa — a hugely damaging disciplinary action that could trouble Lisa's entire life — is similarly disproportionate and unjust, because it is based on unrealistic expectations of her capacities. Further, research shows that punishments are most effective when they are substantial but not severe. Severe punishments can focus children on the unfairness of the punishment and the negative qualities of the adult administering it, distracting them from any moral messages or information that the punishment contains.

But numerous adults are failing to help teenagers find their moral voice for a wholly different reason. Rather than expecting too much of their teenagers, these adults are expecting too little. Especially as parents have come to rely increasingly on teens for closeness over the last few decades, many of us are failing to insist on high standards and important principles—a failure that is abetted by another, opposite myth about adolescence. Over the last few decades, many adults have become acutely aware that adolescence is a distinct developmental stage, influenced in part by a new wave of scientific evidence indicating that the basic circuitry of the teen brain makes them a different animal. I regularly hear parents talk about teenagers as if they are another tribe or species—feral, wholly self-absorbed, amoral. A 1988 *Time* magazine article on childhood put it this way: "Between childhood and adulthood lies the ridiculous and treacherous territory of adolescence. It is a region full of dangers, brainless impulses, hormonal furies." A recent, popular book about adolescence is called *A Tribe Apart.*

Yet it's just as mistaken and risky to view teenagers as a separate species as it is to view them as weak versions of adults, as failed adult clones. The idea that adolescents are differently constructed and beyond the pale has become an easy rationalization for avoiding conflict and failing to hold them to high standards. Fearing conflict, many of us are now too quick to excuse irresponsibility, chalking it up to a "stage." Lisa's mother, in fact, is replicating Lisa's failure in her relationship with Lisa—she is so afraid of angering or alienating Lisa that she is unable to forcefully assert her disappointment with Lisa for failing to tell the truth and to protect the safety of her friend when she observed her drinking heavily, an important principle. (Lisa's mother is also replicating a version of Lisa's dilemma in her relationship with her husband—she can't stand up to him even though she rightfully fears that his right-eousness will drive Lisa away.) When parents are unwilling to withstand their children's anger in the service of promoting a val-ued moral quality in their child, they fail to communicate many critical messages: that there are higher values than being well-liked; that their children are capable of withstanding their disap-proval; and that they themselves, the people their child is supposed to idealize and internalize, are capable of withstanding anger and disdain.

It's a high-wire act, but we as adults need to be able to hold in our heads two seemingly contradictory ideas, an essential irony, about teens—that they are at the same time peer-dependent *and* developing high inner standards. As the Jets sing in "Gee, Officer Krupke": "The trouble is [we're] growing, the trouble is [we're] grown." Research has parsed the many kinds of selves or self-representations that exist in teenagers, including the "actual self," the person you are now; the "ideal self," the kind of person you hope to be; and "ought selves," for example, the person a parent expects you to be (which may or may not greatly overlap with your ideal self). Long ago, the psychoanalyst Anna Freud recognized that behind a great deal of adolescent rebellion was not the lack of conscience but a strengthened, awakened conscience, that teens are pulled by new impulses in ways that war with principles and standards that are also growing stronger. Because teens tend to be aware of what they ought to do and have an "ideal self," they need and respect adults who deeply appreciate their peer predicaments and also ally with their own high inner standards.

That means that Lisa's parents, in addition to commending her for not drinking, should have both expressed their empathy for the very tough situation that she was in and gathered her thinking about why she did what she did. They should have underlined for Lisa the importance of telling the disciplinary board the truth while also acknowledging that the punishment was too severe. They might also have asked, in a welcoming, nondefensive way, why Lisa didn't seek their advice before appearing before the disciplinary board.

And schools, too, need to discipline in ways that reflect the reality of the adolescent self. One could imagine, for example, a school administrator conveying to Lisa an understanding of her dilemma and punishing her more proportionately for her dishonesty—requiring her to help out in the library every week for a semester, for example, or grounding her for several weekends. Further, this administrator might not only reinforce Lisa's sense that honesty is important but enlarge her understanding of why—describing, for example, how lies can add up and unravel the fabric of a school community. And this administrator, rather than remarking sarcastically about Lisa's lack of integrity, might encourage Lisa to talk to her or a counselor if she is again in a situation where the safety of a friend or the safeguarding of an important school principle requires her to "snitch," reassuring Lisa that every effort will be made to protect her friendships in this situation and that the administrator or counselor will take guidance from her about how best to protect these friendships.

We as adults can help teens develop a strong moral core in another sense: we can engage with them in the intricate work of sorting through what to stand up for and when to stand up for it. Adults talk a great deal about the importance of providing children with examples of moral leaders who have deeply sacrificed for principles and about the need to exhort children to rise above peer disapproval. Important as it is for adults to communicate these examples and messages, sticking up for what is right is rarely so straightforward. Even the most morally mature adults routinely struggle to discern whether, when, and how to stand up for their views—whether to take on a boss or colleague who has been unfair, whether to risk the ire of a treasured friend who is mistreating his children, whether and how to talk to a neighbor who is racist or just rude. We all know how hard it is, at any age, to simply be true to oneself—Shakespeare's famous injunction—seductive as that notion is. There is no inner compass that can get us out of every kind of woods. To simply exhort children to stand up for themselves both buries these complexities—it makes these issues only matters of courage and not matters of careful thought and wisdom—and deprives children of access to adult guidance.

We as parents can be far more real and valuable to children if we are able to talk concretely about the balancing of our own needs and the needs of others, about what costs are worth and not worth bearing, about when to adhere to one's conscience and when to accommodate another person's sense of fairness or reality, about how to judge whether one's inclinations are right or whether one is simply too frightened by others' disapproval. We are most effective in these conversations and earn the greatest respect and trust not only when we respect children's thinking and grasp how children make meaning of these situations, but when we can bring our values and wisdom into the context of a child's experience and a child's world. It helps us to understand something in particular about the social dynamics and norms that govern our children's inner and outer lives day to day—to understand, for example, how powerful certain cliques are and what the consequences are of being excluded from them. That's how we can be helpful to teens in dealing with problems they care about—a powerful way of earning their respect. Teens, as the school administrator Laura Rogers observes, can also utterly lose perspective on their peer groups—they can underestimate or greatly overestimate in particular the danger of being excluded—and adults with this understanding can help them step back and develop more realistic, mature insights about these peer situations. It is this delicate integration of guidance, perspective-taking, and assertion, both an authentic connection to who a particular child is and an ability to grasp how that child makes meaning of her experience, an insistence on high standards and an understanding of a child's world—hard as that integration is for any adult—that most effectively nurtures the qualities of the self that are key to moral independence.

Helping teens overcome peer pressure requires one other form

of adult guidance: adults must engage teens in developing principles and moral commitments that are larger than the approval or
disapproval of their peers and larger than themselves. For it is
these commitments that not only make adolescents less vulnerable
to their peers but that can become in adulthood the foundation of
a moral identity and the bedrock of the self.

Some of our great dramas have dealt with how teenagers and
young people can release themselves from the low standards of
others and develop these principles. In the 1950s film *On the Wa-
terfront*, Marlon Brando's Terry Malloy, a man who is guilelessly
subservient to a union mob and still an adolescent in many respects, is provided with an idea of a kind of integrity, an ethic of
responsibility for his community, by a local priest, a higher morality than the dog-eat-dog morality of the streets. Terry testifies
against the mob—he makes snitching honorable—and on the
ground of this new ethic, on this piece of decency, a whole other
life falls into place. He has an answer to the question that tortures
him, the question of whether he is "somebody."

In many respects Terry Malloy's transformation seems quaint.
For in nonreligious communities in this country, we seem to have
lost a sense that a life can be organized, can take its meaning and
shape, from deeply felt principles and commitments. The army
does not recruit by calling to character or stirring idealism. It en-
tices by the promise of being "all that you can be." As psychologist
and researcher William Damon points out, believing in yourself
used to mean believing in your principles; now it means believing
in and advancing your innermost desires. We tend to search for
self-fulfillment, not for a cause that will make the whole idea of
the self seem obsolete. It's the atypical child or young adult these
days who feels that she is "somebody" because she has moral commitments.

But in shifting attention to the needs of the self, we have left
our children in a troubling predicament. Our children are being
pushed to stand up for themselves when the self by itself is a flimsy

thing to stand up for. Rather than focusing narrowly on the dangers of peer pressure, adults should ask themselves whether they are helping children find causes and commitments that are larger than the self that are worth sacrificing for. I am not suggesting something in particular. It could be a broader community—Lisa may have responded very differently to the academic dean's sarcastic remark if she had a deeper commitment to the school community; an ideal worth sacrificing for such as a commitment to end an injustice; a religious commitment to caring for or taking responsibility for others; or just a kind of inner pact to be kind, generous, altruistic. Any of these alone or in combination may give children enough of a sense of self outside their peer group to perhaps at critical moments stop worshiping at the altar of popularity and hold their ground. And this capacity is vital both to children's morality and to their psychological health.

Granted, none of what I'm describing here is simple or straightforward. But it stands a real chance of helping many children become strong and fair adults because it places responsibility where it belongs: not solely on children or their peer groups, but on us, as parents, teachers, and mentors.

2

PROMOTING HAPPINESS *AND* MORALITY

It's around four o'clock, a hazy afternoon gently winding down, and I am with several parents, watching my son's team play basketball in a league game in a nearby town (basketball is a bit of a family obsession). Sitting next to me is Mike, an affable, intense man in his early forties, whom I met at a game earlier in the season. Mike's stepson, Chris, age twelve, is also playing. Chris — lanky, talented — rarely passes the ball, and after weeks of this neglect other kids have become visibly sullen during games. Their resentment seems to have no effect on Mike, who is pumped up that Chris is racking up so many points. I'm debating with myself — should I say something to either Mike or the coach? Mike, though, interrupts my mental wrestling and makes the question moot. He tells me, fairly casually, that a parent of another child on the team has complained to him about Chris not passing. Mike says he's uncomfortable about the comment and does not take it lightly. But he reminds me that Chris has a learning disability and struggles in school. "I'm not going to say anything to him," Mike tells me. "Basketball is so important to him. This is the only place where he can shine."

APPRECIATION

As parents and mentors we are responsible for protecting children from certain destructive feelings such as intense shame. But we are also responsible for cultivating in children certain positive emotions and capacities. And there is a single capacity, as I have argued, at the heart of almost every quality we think of as moral. That is appreciation, the ability to know and value other people, including those different from ourselves in background and perspective. Appreciation not only breaks destructive impulses, this quality is a foundation of the social and emotional skills that comprise the art of treating people well every day, the shadings of decency and respect—the instinct to know how and when to praise and criticize, when to assert oneself and when to listen, how to help without patronizing. Deep knowing and valuing also motivates, even at times compels, moral action. In Huck's refusal to hand over the slave Jim in *Huckleberry Finn*, in flouting the entrenched standards of his time and surrendering to what he sees as a moral weakness in himself, we witness the moral strength of appreciation.

I want to back up a moment to look at the development of empathy—the basis of appreciation. Children are born with certain strong reactions to distress in others. Infants cry, for example, when they hear other infants crying. Yet the extent to which this ability unfolds depends largely on parents' capacity for what some psychologists call "mirroring" and what psychiatrist Daniel Stern calls "attunement." Empathy emerges from parents' warm, responsive attention. When parents are able with some consistency to intuit, track, and reflect back young children's moods and feelings—when a parent beams when a baby squeals in delight, does a quick dance with her hands or head in response to her baby's inner rhythms, or shares a knowing grimace in response to a baby's frustration—children begin to feel deeply reinforcing, empathic connection.

With the right kind of adult guidance, children's empathy begins to evolve into the more complex capacity to appreciate, primarily during the elementary school years. Children need adults who appreciate them, and they also need adults who—unlike Mike in the story above—model appreciation of others and directly guide them in attending to others, including those who may not even be on their radar. Paul, a Chicago parent, recalls teaching his daughter from when she was around four years old to take the perspective of the wait staff in restaurants: "I wanted her to understand that these are real people trying to do a certain job. I wanted to give her ways to respect them and help them do their job better."

Children also learn to appreciate by appreciating us. I am not talking about making our needs the focus. I am talking about requiring children to do basic things like say thank you in response to our generosity, acknowledge our existence in public, express some modicum of interest about major events in our lives, and be mindful of potential burdens or risks we incur. It's important for an eighteen-year-old college student to consider, for example, the legal risks he is creating for his parents if he has a party and a friend brings alcohol. I am also talking about *never* allowing ourselves to be treated as ciphers or doormats. As one parent puts it: "Too often I see teenagers just crap on their parents in front of other people. And their parents just take it. It's shocking."

Children need adults who require them to be helpful, whether it's caring for a younger sibling, getting groceries for a neighbor, or performing routine household chores. Requiring children to be helpful not only builds caring skills but makes attending to others reflexive. They need parents, too, who teach them basic decency. "I was a parent in the late 1960s, and we thought teaching our children manners was bourgeois," one older parent said to me. "And you know what? I learned the hard lesson that if you don't teach your children basic manners, they don't do these things."

Yet many parents are failing to develop empathy in infants or appreciation in older children. There are some fundamentally narcissistic parents who cannot "read" in any meaningful way what a child is experiencing, or they interpret their child's experience entirely in terms of their own history. Some parents are too busy or distracted to enter children's worlds or provide steady, concrete guidance. Some parents were parented so poorly themselves that they have no model in their heads—models of acting and responding that are wired into most adults, that almost magically appear when they become parents—for how to express empathy or create reasonable expectations. These parents often have to battle their own reflexes in order to parent well. Many of them can improve their parenting skills, but they often need one or some combination of therapy or intensive parent education.

THE NEW PARENT TRAP

Yet our research suggests that a larger number of parents—and, paradoxically, many of the most dedicated parents—are failing to nurture appreciation in children for another reason. Every generation of parents has a child-raising mission, and this generation's mission is happiness. (This focus is not entirely new. Many parents in the 1920s and 1930s were focused on children's happiness.) This pursuit is now so fundamental in America that one forgets how ridiculous and entitled it appears to people in many other countries.

There's nothing wrong, of course, with caring about our children's happiness. But making happiness so central can damage children's moral development in many ways. Some parents like Mike are clearly going overboard—they are so bent on promoting happiness that they are failing to help their children develop a basic capacity to tune in to others. Yet the problem is not just a small group of happiness-besotted parents. Many of us, despite our good intentions, in subtle ways put too much emphasis on our children's happiness and too little on their responsibility for others. Many of us slip into habits in the name of promoting happiness—such as regularly monitoring and seeking to adjust our children's moods, organizing our lives too much around our children, and praising them too frequently—that are likely to make children not only less moral but, ironically, less happy.

The good news is that there are certain attributes in the long run that are central to both happiness and many types of moral action—attributes that should be the focus of our parenting. In important respects, we don't have to choose between morality and happiness.

How, concretely, can we avoid overemphasizing our children's happiness at the expense of their goodness? What are the qualities at the root of both happiness and morality, and how can we best promote them?

PULLING BACK ON THE HAPPINESS CAMPAIGN

Our data suggest that across a wide spectrum of cultures and classes, American parents and children view happiness as the main aim of development and place it above other important values. Happiness describes a huge variety of emotional states—the kind of happiness we feel singing along to a stupid song on the radio doesn't have much in common with the gratification we feel when our child makes a close friend. And there are tomes to be written about how different forms of happiness—gratitude, pride, optimism, satisfaction, feelings of competence, passion, wonder—are related to different aspects of morality.

Yet, just to get a rough sense of the weight that children and parents give to happiness in relation to other values, in our research we asked both students and parents to compare the relative importance of being happy, being a "good person who cares about others," achieving at a high level, and having a high-status career. Happiness was the clear winner, and about two-thirds of children ranked their happiness as more important than their goodness. (We asked several children to define happiness, and students used phrases such as "feeling good," "being optimistic," or "feeling satisfied.") We also asked children to imagine how their parents would rank happiness in relationship to these other items. Again happiness was most likely to be ranked first, and about two-thirds of children said their happiness was more important to their parents than their goodness. Another fairly shocking indication that this trend is real is that, according to the Census Bureau, most college freshmen in 1970 said their primary goal was to develop a meaningful life philosophy; in 2005, a version of happiness—"to be comfortably rich"—was college freshmen's primary goal.

A small but significant number of the children we spoke with could be poster children for the vacuous heathenism that some adults point to as proof that the country is going to hell. They didn't seem to care about anything except their happiness: "Happiness is everything," "If you're not happy, nothing else matters," "Being a happy person encompasses everything you want to achieve," "It would be meaningless to be good if I'm not happy."

Yet we found that most parents and children were invested in significant measure in both happiness and goodness, and experienced tension between their own and others' wants and well-being. What was revealing was how this tension was resolved. Some parents and children tell themselves that happiness will lead to goodness—students describe happiness as giving them the motivation and energy to be good. Some students conveyed a life philosophy that can roughly be summarized as this: "Don't worry about giving to others now—get into a good college, make a lot of money, and become financially secure. Then you will be happy and will be able to give to others." It's a version of the oxygen-mask instructions on airplanes: get your mask on first—fill yourself up—and *then* help your neighbor: "My parents see it as cause and effect. If I'm happy and get into a good college, then I'll be able to get a good job and be a positive influence in the world." "I think I will be happier if I go to a good college, and if I'm in a good mood, then I will care more about others." "I would like to change the world, but first I want to secure myself a place in the world. If my position in life enables me to help others, then I would hope I could take advantage of the opportunity."

Only a relatively small number of parents and children thought that goodness or virtue was the key to the development of happiness (an idea frequently connected to the ancient Greek philosophers Epicurus and Aristotle). Some children and parents may also advocate for happiness because they see unhappiness as wholly destructive to morality, as turning people into "scrooges," as one student put it, and some children may simply see no moral benefit to suffering. A high school English teacher who has been teaching for thirty years recently said to me, "My students today are nice and they're smart, but they can't engage suffering in any way. I try to teach them *King Lear*, or 'Letter from Birmingham Jail,' and they just don't want to think about real pain."

While many college students forty years ago used to revel in their suffering, disdaining happiness as shallow, these days a wildly popular course at Harvard University—over eight hundred students—is on the nature of happiness. The study of happiness has become a serious academic discipline—especially the positive-psychology movement led by the University of Pennsylvania's Martin Seligman. Happiness is more likely than suffering to be viewed by young people as a root of morality. Happiness is now deep.

Part and parcel of this intense focus on happiness is another trend. In the last thirty years, Americans have become intoxicated with the power of self-esteem. Self-esteem—championed by dozens of parent advice books, heralded by a 1990 California state task force as a "social vaccine," touted by many teachers—is now widely seen as a linchpin of happiness and an answer to almost every social and moral problem under the sun. The more ludicrous aspects of this trend have prompted a sneering backlash—*Commentary* pages and *Doonesbury* panels alike have lampooned the self-esteem movement as a baleful confluence of liberal indulgence and soft psychology. Yet the attachment to this idea is fierce. In my conversations with parents and teachers around the country, I often hear an almost religious faith in self-esteem's powers. The idea of self-esteem is tremendously arresting in its simplicity and seeming explanatory power, in the gut feeling we have that when we feel good about ourselves, we can do anything, including giving more to others.

These ideas are not baseless. Positive feelings can make people less fragile in the face of conflict or disapproval. They can create hope and more energy to attend to others. All of us can remember times when we've had good news or a gush of good feeling that's made us swell with generosity. Conversely, there are miseries, especially when they are unexamined, from which good rarely comes. Helplessness and hopelessness in particular can be terribly self-occupying and can breed all sorts of destructive behavior.

Yet while it's one thing to say that positive moods can create generosity, it is clearly quite another to view happiness or self-esteem as a long-term foundation for morality. It's important to pause and consider how unique this belief is—that many parents are conveying that happiness or self-esteem leads to morality appears to be unprecedented in American history and may be unprecedented in the history of humankind.

Yet this notion reflects a troubling, impoverished view of morality. For the simple reality is that many vital moral qualities, including strong principles of fairness and justice; the capacity to think through moral problems; appreciation; deeply internalized moral dispositions; the habits of attending to and caring for others and the social and emotional skills needed to treat people well do not spring from happiness or self-esteem. We as parents and mentors can't let ourselves off the hook. We need, intentionally and vigilantly, to cultivate these qualities in our children, assuring that our children practice them day to day.

And the problem is not just parents like Mike but that many of us, because of our entirely natural, strong impulses to promote our children's happiness, can half-consciously place children's happiness over their awareness of others in all sorts of subtle ways that create in them habits and reflexes that are hard to undo.

A few years ago I interviewed a Chicago couple who started bickering halfway through the interview. The mother had allowed the daughter to skip soccer practice because she hadn't felt like playing and was thinking about quitting the team. The father was angry. Staying on the team, he argued, was important for her college resumé. But at some point I realized that neither parent was coming close to another question: what would their daughter's missing practice or quitting mean for the *team?*

Not infrequently, parents fail to help children grasp their responsibility for a community. Often we as parents don't convey to our children that they have obligations to small communities like a sports team or a school choir or a dance troupe. How many of us ever simply mention to our children that a school is not just a place to learn but a community, or that a neighborhood is a community that carries obligations?

Caught up in our children's happiness, we too often let children off the hook when they fail to take responsibility for their peers. At times I found myself, when my children were young, too quick to let them write off friends they found annoying, or failing to insist that they return phone calls from friends, or give credit to other children for their achievements, or reach out to friendless children at the playground. Too often I have seen parents fail to interrupt their children when they talk too much, when they take up too much airtime, either with their friends or with adults. We've all seen parents treat the playground as a battlefield for who gets the most attention, enabling their children at times to be oblivious to other children. I was recently at a playground where a mother allowed her three-year-old to repeatedly pick up a ball that was being used in a game by a group of older children long after these older children understandably stopped finding these disruptions cute.

What makes matters worse is that positive moods can create

real *harm*. Without moral awareness and motivation, contentment and self-satisfaction can infamously breed indifference. Sports fans don't riot when teams lose the championship game, they riot when their team *wins*.

Similarly, while there are certainly problems in conceptualizing and measuring self-esteem, numerous studies reach a similar conclusion: self-esteem, typically defined as a favorable evaluation of oneself, neither deters violence, drug use, and other moral problems, nor does it spark moral conduct. On the contrary, studies show that gang leaders, playground bullies, violent criminals, and delinquents often have high self-esteem and that their high opinion of themselves can make them care not one whit what their victims think. Self-esteem can come in part from feeling powerful, and gang leaders and playground bullies—or high school athletes who abuse their girlfriends—can feel very powerful controlling and degrading others. (As I take up later, gang leaders and bullies may suffer from a fragmented, immature self, but self-esteem and the maturity of the self are quite different.)

But there's another fundamental problem with focusing too much on happiness and self-esteem: it's more likely to make children miserable than happy. The relationship between happiness and morality, to be sure, is highly complex. Self-centered and un-ethical people not only can have high self-esteem, they can at least for a time be quite happy. Yet when parents like Mike place their children's happiness above their awareness of others, children are cheated out of social and moral skills that are key to at least certain kinds of lasting well-being. These children are not being prepared for the other-centeredness that's fundamental to long-term, healthy relationships, to being a good spouse, parent, friend, or mentor. That's one reason the direct pursuit of happiness so predictably produces unhappiness. "Those only are happy," John Stuart Mill wrote, "who have their minds fixed on some object other than their own happiness." Many American parents are now paying for a lazy and reckless bet. As Darrin McMahon observes in a recent book on the history of happiness, the disappointment of adults these days is that we have forsaken nobility—our culture no longer places a high premium on virtue—but have not obtained the happiness that we expected would replace it.

A final note on the happiness conundrum. A small but significant number of parents and children we spoke with, as I noted, were less convinced that happiness leads to goodness than that goodness leads to happiness—the Aristotelian idea. I have talked to teachers and coaches who propagate the idea that the rewards of goodness will be reaped in greater happiness. A new book— *Why Good Things Happen to Good People*—even promotes the idea that being a good person is the key to health and a longer life.

Yet while it's too simple and misdirected to say that happiness will lead to goodness, it's also too simple—and can be harmful—to say that goodness will lead to happiness. Good people can clearly be miserable. Standing up for important principles or for friends, for example, may bring painful ostracism. To expect morality to make us happy, to tell children to be good because it will make them feel good, is to violate a core element of morality—our obligations to others for their own sake, our responsibility to do what's right whether or not it's helpful or harmful to us. While we ought, then, to tell our children that certain kinds of goodness can be rewarding, we should not tell them to be good or moral simply because it will make them happy. We should tell our children to be moral because it is moral, because it is vital to our collective good, and because the well-being of others is as important as their own.

"It came to me pretty suddenly one day that parenting is a moral task," a Chicago parent starkly put it, "that the principle of being a mother of a child who is a good person is more important than how much my kids like me or how happy they are in the moment. If my kids were going to be good people, I realized that I couldn't go to them all the time if they cried or always be a fixer or problem solver, that I had to make real demands on them."

There is a great deal we can do to shift away from our narrow focus on happiness. In our interviews we found at least some parents open to questioning their happiness focus. Most of us as parents have a knee-jerk reaction when asked what we want for our children: we say we just want them to be happy. But when asked to justify that view, some parents begin to question whether happiness is more important than goodness or whether their children's happiness was too big a factor in their parenting. One parent e-mailed me after our interview because she had changed her mind: "I thought about your question after you left, and my kids' happiness is really not what's most important to me. What's most important is that they're thoughtful in whatever they do, that they think, reflect, and care." Other parents, such as the parent above, have moments in the course of parenting when they see that their children's happiness is inconsistent with their highest values, and they seize these moments. More of us as parents can be alert to these moments. We can, too, realize that feeling tension between meeting our children's needs and meeting other children's needs on a playground or a sports team—and having our children experience that tension—is not a bad thing. That tension is, in fact, at the heart of being a moral person.

Instead of following our reflex to tell our children over and over that "we just want you to be happy," it also doesn't require a great deal more effort for us explicitly to value kindness in children as much as we value happiness. (William James allegedly said on his deathbed that there are only three important things in life: kindness, kindness, and kindness.) We can also work to assure that our own desire for happiness is not tacitly compromising our children's morality. In investing so much in Chris performing well at basketball, Mike may be protecting his own happiness over Chris's morality and happiness.

In the big picture, though, the fundamental challenge is for us to rethink our basic parenting goals and to focus on qualities that are likely to promote both happiness and morality, a topic I take up later in this chapter.

MOOD POLICING AND THE PRAISE CRAZE

A few years ago at a school picnic I wound up in a conversation with a mother who introduced herself as Nancy. At some point in the conversation I mentioned to Nancy that I was a psychologist, and she spilled out her concerns about her five-year-old daughter, Shana. Shana seemed to have difficulty playing with other children and had few friends. She expected other children to gravitate toward her and to be interested in what she was interested in. I asked whether Shana seemed happy at home, and Nancy told me that, in part because Shana was having trouble making friends, Nancy went to great lengths to ensure that Shana didn't experience any distress at home. Later in the conversation she related, laughing with some discomfort, that she'd been late to work that day because she had to return to her bedroom twice to change: "Shana didn't like my outfits."

It's clearly troubling that many parents are putting their children's happiness and self-esteem before their moral development. Yet what's just as damaging to children's moral and emotional growth are the parenting practices this focus has spawned. Some adults these days, like Nancy, believe that the best way to shore up their children's happiness and self-esteem is not only to shield them from suffering but to cater to their every need and to remove from their lives even tiny burdens. Many of us in more subtle ways—I certainly have to monitor myself in this—overprotect our children or act as their servants.

I am not simply joining the chorus of cultural observers decrying parental indulgence. (There's even a new name for these parents—*dimpies*—short for "doting indulgent modern parents.") Much of what is commonly called indulgence is absolutely harmless to children, or even beneficial. Parents do *not* indulge their children, for example, when they give them input into decisions affecting their lives, respect their opinions, or place their needs before their own. Lavishing attention on young children is not the problem: it's very hard to indulge a one-year-old. That more parents are doing these things is a very encouraging aspect of modern parenting.

On the other hand, when parents like Nancy organize their entire lives around their children in the name of shielding them from discomfort—when they place their children's trivial preferences before their own significant needs, such as getting to work on time—they make it more likely that their children will expect others to organize their lives around them. Similarly, when we as parents get in the habit of doing small things to make our children's lives easier—when we clean up after them, drive them places that they could walk to, fill out applications for our teenagers, pay teenagers' parking tickets, or regularly jump in to solve children's problems with peers, teachers, or coaches—we run the risk of making our children more fragile, entitled, and self-occupied. When Diane, a parent of a college freshman, suggests that her daughter, who doesn't want to have a roommate, lie to the dean of the college—falsely claiming she has a respiratory illness—she is not only placing little value on honesty, she is making her daughter's feelings too precious, patronizing her, and utterly failing to help her daughter understand how this kind of self-interest erodes the basis for community. The now legendary, herculean lengths to which some parents go to spare their children disappointments, rejections, and losses—whether it's losing a sporting event, not being accepted into a valued club or team, or being rejected by a friend—are acts of care that can make children care less about everything except themselves.

And there are other parenting trends intended to secure children's happiness that are positive in moderation but can become excessive, undermining moral growth. Some parents are so focused, for instance, on keeping their children entertained at every moment—our generation of parents, research suggests, may be more invested than any generation of parents in history in entertaining their children virtually every moment, from birth until age eighteen—that they may fail to make demands on their children, including requiring them regularly to do household chores, or to help out neighbors.

Many parents are trying to safeguard children's well-being by asking their children about their feelings and noting their moods. For example, a parent, in telling a five-year-old child that it's time to leave a swimming pool and go home, will say: "I know you feel disappointed." This trend is also positive and heartening in many respects. These parents, unlike those of previous generations, are rightly concerned about children's—especially boys'—capacity to identify and express their feelings. Often these parents know, from observing their own parents, that bottling up or being disconnected from one's feelings impairs one's relationships and is a significant mental health risk—and that knowing and appropriately articulating one's feelings is a hallmark of mature relationships and effective participation in any group or community. And I have seen parents do this noting of moods and asking about feelings in very healthy ways.

Yet I have seen parents in the course of a couple of hours ask children several times how they are feeling or repeatedly remark on their moods. "You must be feeling tired." "That must be frustrating for you." "That must make you sad." This kind of constant monitoring can make children's transient feelings too important and be stultifying, irritating, and intrusive: it's like pulling a bandage off a wound every five minutes to see if it's healing, or pulling a plant up every few minutes to see if it's growing. Often this running commentary pushes children away from their parents, eroding parents' emotional and moral influence.

Not infrequently, I also come across parents who, in the name of protecting their children's happiness, treat children's feelings as if these feelings are at every moment on trial for their lives. They worry, for instance, that any insult or perceived betrayal will permanently damage a child's trust, or that temporarily being excluded by a clique will destroy a child's self-esteem. Yet these worries also patronize children, conveying a dismal assessment of their capacities, and this attentiveness can cause children to dramatize their feelings, to once again make their feelings too precious. Children become so involved in their own inner theaters and so busy asking themselves how they are doing that they aren't naturally aware of other children.

Praising children in the service of happiness and self-esteem is yet another omnipresent parenting practice, and once again this trend has important benefits. Children thrive on praise, research shows, when it is sincere and connected to specific accomplishment — instead of telling children over and over that they are smart, better to point to a specific improvement on a paper or an exam. And it certainly can be reinforcing to praise specific moral acts. Every child can also benefit from praise that isn't connected to specific accomplishment but reflects a more general sense of who they are. Children should be told at times that they are "great" or "terrific."

Yet praising, too, can become excessive. Constant praising has become background noise on countless suburban playgrounds. I recently watched a father playing catch with his son, and he complimented every single one of his catches and throws (when his son flat-out dropped the ball, he said "nice try"). Programs in schools designed to promote social, emotional, or moral development often rely heavily on praise. One highly respected and popular children's sports character-education program that is otherwise quite sensible recommends that parents find some reason to praise their children *five* times for every time they criticize them — an approach to praise that is both excessive and far too robotic, oblivious to the nuances of when and how to praise usefully.

Children also tend to know when they have really accomplished something and when they have not, and too much unconditional praise or frequent praise that is connected to tiny achievements can create self-doubts and cynicism about adults, undermining adults as mentors. Children often start to wonder why adults need to constantly prop them up. As psychologist William Damon points out, "Children are perfectly capable of asking the same questions that we would ask when faced with empty flattery: 'Why do people think they need to make things up about me? What is wrong with me that people need to cover up? What are these stories about me trying to prove?'" Psychologist and researcher Wulf-Uwe Meyer uncovered that by the age of twelve, children often view praise from a teacher as a sign that they lack ability and that teachers think that they need extra encouragement. Other research on praise suggests that children who are praised too much become more conscious of their image, more competitive, and more prone to cut others down. When children are praised all the time, they can also feel judged all the time — they may feel that their competence is always on the line, making them vulnerable to shame and other negative self-assessments. And too much praise can hook children on praise — children can start to require higher and higher doses of compliments and may feel that there is something wrong with them when they aren't being bombarded with kudos.

Too much global praise — when kids are frequently told that they are "great" or "terrific" — creates particular dangers. Such praise can train children to think that their essential value, their entire worth, is the issue in many contexts. Their selves always at stake, these children are prone to inflate their importance, both positively and negatively. The self acquires false credit and false dues, and these children can develop, as the psychologist Robert Karen notes, both a distorted, narcissistic picture of their value and a high vulnerability to shame.

In all these ways, then, when adults believe that the more they praise and the higher the praise, the better children will feel — when they treat the self like a tank that should be filled to the brim — they are, in fact, depleting children's inner resources. Again, the irony is that all this work to buttress self-esteem and happiness not only makes children less capable of moral action — more self-occupied, less able to invest in others, more fragile, and less able to stand up for important values—but more likely to fret about their attractiveness, competence, or importance to others, more prone to worry and unhappiness.

There is much that we can do to avoid these pitfalls. We can work to treat children's daily distresses as unalarming. We can avoid intervening preemptively with a peer, teacher, or coach and make a habit instead of enabling children to solve problems and conflicts and to accomplish tasks on their own. A few rules of thumb can help. While it's important at times to directly coach toddlers and preschool children around peer issues, we should avoid unsolicited coaching of older children, with the exception of addressing possible physical harm or outright cruelty—or in those instances when a child has recurring or serious peer problems. Similarly, it's important for parents to step in to help resolve children's conflicts with teachers and coaches only when those conflicts are large and when children clearly can't resolve them themselves. While it usually doesn't make sense to intervene, for example, when a child feels that she is sometimes treated unfairly by a teacher or coach or is not as well liked by a teacher or coach as other children, it is certainly appropriate to get involved if there's a long-standing pattern of unfairness, when children are frequently in conflict with these adults or when these adults are clearly putting their own needs before children's. Although I didn't take action when one of my son's high school teachers, for example, sometimes criticized his work in ways that seemed silly and harsh, I quickly intervened when this teacher criticized my son and other students for going behind her back and talking to a guidance counselor about their struggles in this class—a clear example of her protecting herself at the expense of her students.

If we want children to be articulate about their troubling feelings, we don't need to name for them every momentary feeling; instead, we should help children identify and talk about these feelings when they are prolonged and when children solicit our input. It's also helpful for us to develop a basic understanding of what kinds of feelings children are able to express at different developmental stages, of how boys and girls differ in how they experience and express various emotions and to work hard to model the appropriate expression of feelings ourselves. My twelve-year-old daughter and I have similar anxieties, and I work hard to talk about my worries, for example, only when it seems relevant and meaningful to her and in ways that help her cope. I tell her, for example, that worrying has a strong biological basis—it's not an indication of weakness—and I share with her strategies I've used to manage anxiety. It's also important in most cases to avoid—when children are temporarily angry at us—being both a parent (a legitimate object of anger) and a therapist (someone who is "naming" or analyzing the feelings of anger). As psychologist Janina Fisher observes, it can be confusing for a child when a parent takes both these roles, and it can prevent them from working through their anger toward us on their own terms.

To break the praise craze, it will help if parents use global praise only occasionally—if they generally connect their praise to specific accomplishment. It's also important to sense how a particular child experiences praise. Some children feel instinctively patronized by praise, while other children are praise sponges. The first type of child may need help accepting compliments, while the second type may need help living without them.

What may be most helpful in reducing harmful praise, though, is if we as parents are able to reflect on *why* we are constantly praising our children. In our highly psychological culture, our inflated concerns about our children's emotional vulnerabilities—and in some cases our keen sense of the ways in which we were emotionally cheated as children—can drive this praising. Because praising can create dependence, it serves some parents' need for closeness and control. The constant praising of children is also, for many busy and stressed adults, a shortcut, a seemingly easy substitute for their inability to pay sufficient attention to a child. Yet time and real engagement are meaningful to a child—"time is how you spend your love," the novelist Zadie Smith writes—in a way that "you're terrific" is not. Sometimes isolated, recognition-deprived parents may also be projecting onto children their own need for recognition and praise. Recognizing these motivations is often the first, key step for us in engaging—and praising—our children in healthier ways.

A NEW GOAL FOR PARENTS

Important as these steps are, what will be most important is for us to fundamentally shift our parenting goals. For there are qualities that are likely to promote enduring well-being and key moral qualities—qualities that tend to drift off our radar—that should be the main focus of our parenting. These qualities include the ability to balance and coordinate our needs with others, to be reflective and self-critical—to fairly and generously assess our behavior—to receive feedback constructively, and to change our behavior based on our own and others' assessments. These qualities also include, as I described in the last chapter, the ability to manage destructive feelings. It is these capacities that enable children and adults to appreciate others despite conflicts of interest and differences in perspective, to adhere to important principles and to engage in sturdy, meaningful relationships and endeavors that create lasting self-worth. These are the ingredients of what we call *maturity,* and they reflect the strength and integrity of the self. It's important to remember here that self-esteem and the strength or maturity of the self are quite different, yet they are often confused, a confusion that stems from the fact that our vocabulary of the self is so impoverished, our language about the self so crude and vague. Though some violent children have high self-esteem, the self that is being esteemed is immature, incapable of empathy, unable to integrate others' needs with its own, unaware of itself, unable to control intense feelings.

As parents we nurture our children's healthy maturity in many different ways, but the following practices are most central:

1. The self becomes stronger and more mature less by being praised than by being *known*. That means that it's important that our interactions with our children generally reflect our knowledge of them. This knowledge should be reflected when we choose an activity for them, talk to them about their day, help them solve a personal problem. It's important, too, that we are able to reflect back to children at key moments something about who they are — not a steady stream of observations but an occasional knowing observation about a particular quality. We might take note, for example, of tasks that come easily to them, challenges they seem to avoid, or things that capture their interest or bore them.

2. Children come to be reflective and self-critical chiefly when we encourage their self-observations and when we model for them honest self-reflection. It is by dealing insightfully and candidly with our own flaws that we give children permission and a map to engage those qualities about themselves that they find troubling. A father I know, for example, talked to his children about his being too critical of other people. In that single reflection, this father reduced the stigma his children may feel in talking about a weakness, informed his children about a quality that he does *not* intend to model, and encouraged them to reflect on the fairness of their own assessments of others and on whether they have the same flaw.

3. When we demonstrate a capacity to change a troubling behavior as a result of our self-reflections, or as a result of feedback, we model a vital aspect of maturity. We also express a critical form of respect for children and other family members who are often most hurt by these behaviors.

One single mother I know, Beth, told me about a time, after a long and stressful day, when her ten-year-old daughter broke a glass while setting the table. Beth rolled her eyes and sighed in disgust at the mess, at which her daughter burst into tears and said, "You are always so mean when you're making dinner!" Beth, immediately remorseful, told her daughter that she'd been having a tough time at work—that a new perfectionist boss was expecting too much of her—and that she realized that that pressure was making her irritable and causing her to do with her daughter exactly what the boss was doing to her—expect too much. Beth apologized, told her daughter that she was right to give this feedback, and "promised to leave the perfectionism to her boss."

4. Among the many ways that children learn to deal with difficult feelings such as frustration and anger is when we model the appropriate expression of these emotions and don't let our own frustration and anger corrode our relationships with our children. When I'm angry at my children, I have a tendency at times to stew. I thus try hard to express anger in simple, clear terms and to reestablish some connection with them fairly quickly, as Beth above also does, after I show anger or after a fight.

5. Another critical way children learn to control hostile feelings toward others, as well as coordinate their needs with others, as I take up in chapter 6, is by developing the ability to take a third-person perspective, stepping outside

a relationship. We can, specifically, ask children to imagine how they would handle a difficult situation if they were "being their best self," or to imagine how a person they admire would handle this situation.

OUR CHILDREN'S HUMANITY

Finally, there may even be something beyond the self, more fundamental and deeper, that many American parents hardly think about at all. If we are concerned about our children's morality, we ought to be thinking carefully about their humanity. I am speaking of the experience of deep vitality, meaning, and compassion generated by an awareness that we are distinct expressions of common roots across time and space, that we are intimately and intricately connected to other human beings, both living and dead. It is no accident that so many of our great thinkers have feared a morality untethered to some larger sense of humanity or faith. In Dostoevsky's *The Brothers Karamazov*, Ivan Karamazov famously contends that if there is no God, everything is permitted. This sense of humanity charges us with responsibility—a sense of what we owe not only the living but those who have lived before us and those who will live after we are gone. But in nonreligious communities few parents are cultivating humanity in children by careful talk about the dead, by helping their children connect their experiences to the experiences of other children in other cultures, by reflecting with them about their responsibility for future generations. It may seem difficult and awkward for many of us as parents, outside of a religious setting, to have these kinds of talks. But children can develop this sensibility in many ways—when we, for example, ask respectful and searching questions of others from other cultures in the presence of our children, when we read and reflect on literature together with our children, when we help them make sense of current events by drawing lessons from history.

It may seem like a tall order to change our parenting goals, to change these fundamental conceptions of the self, or to cultivate in children an expansive sense of humanity. But it's worth noting that adulation of the self is a distinctly modern phenomenon and has occupied a tiny place in our history—it was not until the nineteenth century that the sense of the self became significant, and not until the last thirty years or so that liking oneself became such a value for its own sake. Parenting goals have fluctuated, sometimes dramatically, throughout history. The question is not whether parenting goals can change. It is whether we can summon the wisdom and discipline to direct that change, and how soon.

3

THE REAL DANGER IN THE ACHIEVEMENT CRAZE

IT IS EARLY EVENING, and I am speaking to a group of about forty parents at a high-powered and well-respected independent school with a stunning record for passing students on to prestigious colleges. The topic is moral development, and one reason I have been asked to speak is concern among both faculty and parents that an intense focus on academic achievement at the school has squeezed out attention to other crucial aspects of kids' lives. About fifteen minutes into my talk, a hand shoots up and a parent asks this question: "I agree with you that it's important for kids to be good people, but, realistically, you're asking us to focus on our children being good people when it won't help my child get into a place like Harvard." Another parent quips: "Can you change Harvard so that being a good person counts in the application?" Most parents in the audience are laughing slightly and nervously. But some parents seem on the edge of their seats—how much should they focus on their child being good? Will it help their child get accepted at a prestigious school?

Increasingly in recent years I have heard stories about children in private schools and wealthy suburban schools who are strung-out achievement junkies and about parents who drive them relentlessly. I have mostly chalked the stories up to the typical ways some parents cluck about other parents, magnifying other parents' flaws so that they can feel that their own parenting and their own kids are somehow purer and better. Wealthy parents are also, of course, easy targets. They seem to have no excuses and few defenders.

And I have found many parents in these schools who have entirely healthy attitudes about their children's achievements—parents who are simply trying to fathom the mystery of what makes their children tick and what will make them thrive. And I have met many kind, emotionally healthy, and well-grounded children in these schools. Images in popular culture of rich kids as morally imbecilic, trust fund–pampered, Porsche-driving vipers are as wildly off-target as are stereotypes of marauding, gun-toting, crack-addled poor black and Latino kids.

But the fact remains: many parents today are simply craven about academic achievement. That parents would make unabashed comments like those above in a public forum is a telling indication of how mainstream this intensity about high achievement is in certain communities.

Parents in affluent communities and in many middle-class communities are now going to legendary lengths to launch this achievement project, starting at birth. Games and video programs that seek to prime the mental engines of infants and toddlers, with slogans like "Turn game time into brain time," are proliferating wildly—a third of American children have seen a Baby Einstein video. Some parents not only become paramilitary when it comes to securing selective preschool slots but procure tutors for their preschool children.

Yet it's clearly when college looms on the horizon that the true madness begins. As a recent *Atlantic Monthly* article observed, "*millions* of families are now in a state of nervous collapse regarding college admissions," and large numbers of kids are in terror that if they don't get into a high-profile college, their life, as a long-time college-admissions consultant puts it, is "ruined." In our private-school survey, about 40 percent of students identified getting into a "good college" as more important than being a "good person," and nearly one-half of students said that it was more important to their parents that they get into a good college than that they be good people. When I shared this data with staff of this private school, a few teachers protested vehemently. They thought these numbers were too *low:* "The kids are lying to you. All that parents here care about is getting their kids into a good college." "The pressure to do well is up. The demand to do good is down, way down," a recent *New York Times* article announces, "particularly if it's the kind of do-gooding that doesn't show up on a college application." The parental harping on academic achievement has become so blatant that it has created a backlash of parent-mocking bumper stickers and pins with slogans like, "My kid sells term papers to your honors student," "My kid beat up your honors student," and "My kid is a retard at the Lincoln School."

Yet tempting as it is to focus on achievement-obsessed parents, the more pervasive problem is far more subtle. The problem is not simply "them." If we are honest, many of us have intense feelings about our children's achievement that we haven't quite dealt with squarely. Some of us are quietly organizing our relationships with our children around their achievements and making children's high achievements the main, if unspoken, focus of our parenting. And this focus can set children up for misery and threaten the development of exactly those qualities of the self that are the basis of appreciation, integrity, and caring.

What's more, many of us are inadvertently sending our children all sorts of double messages about the importance of achieving at high levels—telling children that high achievement doesn't matter, say, while communicating in a thousand covert ways that achievement matters very much. I have heard countless cocktail party conversations among parents who are anguished about being hypocritical or lying to their children about their own drug use in their youth. But I've never been in a conversation among parents about how to avoid double messages regarding an issue that is more layered and far larger—how to speak authentically and with integrity to our children about achievement.

The point is not, of course, that parents should stop putting pressure on their children to achieve. It is entirely possible for children to achieve stratospherically and at the same time to lead lives of great integrity and compassion. Yet how can we deal with our own confused, sometimes irrational feelings about achievement, so that we can talk to our children honestly and constructively? How can we make achievement for our children not the prime way they measure their value but only one theme in the larger composition of a life?

THE DAMAGE: EMOTIONAL AND MORAL

"There are parents here who make a bargain with their kids," Dan Shawn, a high school counselor, tells me. "The tacit contract is this: If you get good grades, I don't care what you do. You can party hard, you can drink, you can have parties when I'm not home. And these are the kids I end up seeing in my office—they're the ones who are in trouble."

"When I met Sara," Sara's therapist tells me, "she was twenty-two years old and she had no idea who she was. She had been like a performance machine. Her parents seemed to dread what would happen if Sara didn't do very well in everything she did. But I don't think she was ever able to figure out what she wanted. She was angry and adrift and empty and she didn't know why. The work of therapy is very slowly helping her start over and figure out what she wants, who she is. She's having to go back and create a self."

Recent research by Columbia University psychologists Suniya Luthar and Shawn Latendresse suggests something striking and troubling: even though poor children face many hardships, teenagers in affluent families are suffering emotional and moral problems at roughly the same rates as poor children. The causes of these troubles, to be sure, clearly differ in rich and poor communities—as do the consequences. Yet affluent children suffer high rates of behavior problems, delinquency, drug use (including hard drugs), anxiety, and depression—suburban girls are three times more likely to report clinical levels of depression than other teens on average.

There is no single explanation for these troubles. Some children's lack of contact with parents in affluent communities, the absence of community ties in many affluent neighborhoods, and parental indulgence may all play a part. These troubles may worsen because many affluent families, as mentioned earlier, worry about how they are perceived—worries that cause them to bury problems and eschew needed help. Some teachers and other professionals working with these children may also be less inclined to take their troubles seriously, so children don't receive adequate support and understanding. As one teacher said to me: "I worked in poor schools and then in rich schools, and when I got to the rich schools I had kids breaking down all the time, crying in class about little things. And I remember asking myself: 'How hard can your life be?' It just seemed so overdramatic."

But the link between these troubles and achievement pressures, according to these researchers, is clear and strong. Children with "very high perfectionist strivings—those who saw achievement failures as personal failures"—appear to be more at risk for almost all of these troubles, as are those children whose parents put too much weight on their accomplishments, valuing them more than aspects of their character.

Part of the blame for these troubles lies with private and suburban schools, where achievement pressures and competition can be brutal. Some children, to be sure, flourish under intense competitive pressure, and other children certainly need outside pressure in order to push through challenging academic tasks. The mountain of literature deploring academic pressure and competition in school is often oblivious both to the complexity of achievement motivation and to vast differences in the way children experience competition. Yet in some schools, these pressures have clearly rocketed out of control. In our research in one private school, many children described poignantly their struggles to be honest, generous, and caring, and to see others as more than mere impediments to their goals. "I have to lie to kids here about my [low] GPA so they won't look down on me." "I get so stressed out and irritable about all the pressure here to get good grades that sometimes I'm a jerk." "Kids here say that they would help someone out rather than work hard, but they're lying." "I'm tempted to gloat to the person next to me when I get a good grade rather than help them understand."

Yet there's no question that children feel the most heat to achieve—and, more important, develop their understandings of what high achievement is and why it is important—from their parents. And it's very clear that many parents are sending messages about achievement that are damaging children's moral growth. Some of this damage is unnervingly obvious, as when some parents convey to their children in both explicit and unspoken ways that their accomplishments and attending a good college are more important than being a good person, or tell their children that if they obtain good grades that they can "party hard." Crassly ambitious for their children, some parents are failing to model a basic sense of equity and fairness. We interviewed parents of one high school junior in a New York suburb who had set up a vocational school in a South American country in part so that their daughter could say in her college application that she had started a school in a developing country. I have heard about parents paying jaw-dropping amounts of money—several thousand dollars a year—for their children's SAT tutors, beginning in *fifth* grade. It's not rare in affluent communities for parents to get a psychiatrist to falsely diagnose their child as having attention deficit disorder (ADD) because these children get more time on the SATs. As one parent I spoke with who aggressively pushes her children put it, "It's incredibly competitive out there and I don't want my child left in the dust."

Yet this damage is less pervasive than the harm done to children by parents who are intensely promoting their children's achievements in more quiet, often unexamined ways.

I have argued that children come to appreciate and care for others and to stand for important principles when parents not only stand for important principles and standards but know and value their children, including what is distinctive about them. It is this kind of appreciation that strengthens the self and helps children develop maturity, including the ability to disentangle their needs from others', to value thoughts and feelings that are different from their own, and to form and assert independent views. Yet when parents, like Sara's parents, are narrowly focused on performance or simply place their children's academic achievement above other values—quietly pressuring their children, for example, to take courses and to participate in extracurricular activities in which they have no interest because it will help them get into good colleges, or constantly arranging achievement-boosting activities, or encouraging them to apply to prestigious colleges where they are unlikely to fit in and thrive—children may not be known or valued for the qualities they know and prize in themselves. A child who is socially skilled, deeply loyal, honest, funny, feisty, caring, imaginative, or vibrant—among many, many qualities—may never come to value these qualities or see them as anywhere near the core of her being. In these circumstances, children are also more likely to view others simply in terms of their achievements and to see them as competitors or threats to their own achievements. They suffer both a diminished sense of others and a diminished sense of themselves.

Some children also come to understand that their parents' admiration and affection are conditioned on high achievement and that to fail is to lose love. "There are children who are simply suffering here because they feel they're not achieving enough," a high school dean of students at a high-powered private school tells me. "And their parents will do anything for them—get them psychiatrists, tutors, fancy afterschool activities—except tell them what they need to hear most: 'I love you no matter how much you achieve.'" As Alice Miller describes in her classic book on achievement pressures, *The Drama of the Gifted Child*, under these circumstances children learn to carefully closet their feelings, convinced that their parents cannot tolerate feelings such as anxiety, anger, and sadness that may impede their performance. These children have less capacity to identify feelings in themselves and in others, and they are far more likely to suffer the distrust of their own feelings and the chronic neediness and sense of deficiency, what Luthar and Latendresse call a "meager sense of self," that makes it hard to invest in others and to remain unswayed in the face of the unthinking whims of peers. What I hear from both teachers and counselors in schools with middle- and upper-class children is far less concern about children being malicious than about their being unquestioning, blindly dutiful, anxious to please. When children have to closet feelings because they see them as unwanted and illegitimate, when they dread the disapproval of their parents when they fail or simply are not superstars, shame, as I described in chapter 1, can also become a core, hounding aspect of the self. Because some children like Sara have so internalized achievement pressures, they also can find themselves ashamed and angry at their parents without knowing why, and they wind up ashamed of this shame and anger as well. Charles Ducey, a psychologist who was the head of a counseling clinic at Harvard University for many years, told me that he "saw students all the time who just hated themselves for not succeeding, for not getting a great grade in a course, and they had no idea why they were so hard on themselves."

KIDDING OURSELVES

A few years ago I was talking with a levelheaded, worldly sixteen-year-old in our neighborhood, Jim Martin, whose parents I respect a great deal. Jim describes himself as having an open and honest relationship with his parents—except when it comes to their expectations about his achievement. "My parents tell me all the time that getting into a high-status college isn't a big deal, that they're more interested in my learning and going to a college where I'm happy. But then they pay for SAT prep courses and expensive college counselors. And the fact is that my parents don't have to say anything about how important it is and I'm still going to feel a lot of pressure to go to one of these places. They went to great schools, and they know that all my older cousins have gone to places like Stanford and Princeton. The only reason they can tell themselves they're not pressuring me is that there's already huge pressure on me to achieve."

In talking to dozens of high school students and college undergraduates and graduate students over the last several years, I came across another threat to children's moral growth created by achievement pressure. Many young people are not passively imbibing their parents' and teachers' messages about achievement at all. They are, like Jim, quite keen observers, in fact, of their parents' and other adults' "talk" about achievement, and they see these adults as engaging in various forms of double-dealing and hypocrisy. In one respect, young people who are critical about these achievement pressures are better off. They are displaying "a capacity for perspective," as Charles Ducey observes, "that reflects a more developed sense of self." Yet their awareness can also create large fractures in their trust in their parents and teachers as moral mentors.

In the eyes of some young people, there is a glaring gulf between what many teachers and school administrators say and do. These students complain that school staff frequently, as one suburban high school student put it, "give lip service" to character, "but when it comes down to it, all they really care about is our grades." I talked to several students at a high-powered private school who felt, in this case with some justification, that school administrators talked the talk about character but only took action—lectured them about sexual responsibility or "beat into [our] heads the importance of not driving drunk"—when they worried about a calamity that would provoke a lawsuit.

Yet what I have heard about most is various forms of parental hypocrisy. Some young people simply see their parents as fooling themselves about how much achievement matters to them. Another interviewee told me that when he got to college he tortured his parents, who made a big show of not caring about his grades, by withholding his grades from them—"I'd just be quiet on the phone and make them ask." High school student Ariel Karlin wrote in *U.S. News & World Report*'s annual issue ranking America's colleges: "My mother delights in anecdotes about the ridiculous activities of the 'psycho moms,' her name for mothers who are overly anxious about where their children will attend college. This is how she reassures herself that she is not as crackers as these women."

Young people, like Jim Martin, can feel in particular that their parents have fooled themselves into thinking that they aren't harping on achievement because communities or extended families or schools are doing the achievement hammering and muscling for them. Other students report that one parent sends one message and another parent sends a contradictory message, or that parents vacillate wildly between pushing achievement and downplaying it, or that parents are "really anxious" and accidentally let their "emotions show." Still other students receive messages from parents that are designed to take the pressure off but don't take the pressure off at all. One parent we interviewed said, without a trace of irony, that while it was very important to her that her children go to great colleges, her husband felt differently. He would be happy if their children ended up at a place like Swarthmore (a highly competitive, superb school), "which is a good school, but not an Ivy."

Some parents try to resolve the conflict by falling back on simple maxims. Yet these maxims can also make them seem hypocritical in the eyes of their children. As parents, we may say, for instance, that we are harping on achievement because we want our children to have a wide array of career options. That's a natural impulse. Many of us want our children to go to elite high schools or colleges so that they will have a better shot at being a doctor or lawyer or corporate leader. We know that high-paying, high-status jobs can bring all sorts of advantages that cannot be understood from the vantage point of childhood.

But young people may come to question what kind of choices they are really being given if they are sent to schools where the culture of academic achievement is fierce. Some young people don't feel they have the option of entering a whole array of careers—whether teaching, forestry, carpentry, or firefighting—that may be more aligned with their wants. "I told my daughter that I thought she needed to apply herself in school because I wanted her to have options as an adult," a mother from a high-achieving family, living in a high-achieving community, said, "and she said to me, 'Are you giving me the option to be a beautician?'" Ariel Karlin writes that her parents have always said that she could be whatever she wanted, but "I doubt mom and dad would be very enthusiastic if I decided that my true calling was to be an alpaca farmer in Peru. Of course, if I asked to take an expensive extracurricular workshop teaching leadership skills in Peruvian alpaca farming, my parents would have me signed up faster than you can say 'deranged.' Anything to build my college resume."

Some parents, our survey suggests, fall into another kind of contradiction that can erode children's faith in them. Parents say they just want their children to "maximize their abilities," to "live up to their potential," while at the same time stressing that their children's happiness is most important to them. While it seems sensible to want children to maximize their abilities, at some point it can dawn on children that maximizing their abilities may not make them happy—that we as parents are not talking about working at something that they love at a pace that feels comfortable to them. Similarly, when parents continually push children to excel in academic areas in which they have a talent but that they don't naturally enjoy—whether math or science or art—children can sniff out that their happiness is not really the goal. At some point, again, many children become aware of the gulf that separates what parents are saying and what parents really expect of them.

My point is not, though, that we as parents should beat ourselves up for being hypocritical. It's terrifically difficult to know how to talk to children about achievement, and many parents are clearly and honestly struggling—I know I struggle—with the contradictions in their messages. Of all the questions I ask parents, the one about how they talk to their children about high achievement clearly hits a nerve and taps into a mother lode of ambivalent, buried feeling. When I asked one parent about what he says to his child about achievement, he laughed knowingly and uncomfortably and replied, "You go first!" as if I had asked him about his sex life or drug use. He added: "I don't know how *I* feel about achievement. How am I possibly going to convey helpful messages to my kids?" Other parents are aware of the conflict between focusing on high achievement and saying that happiness is most important: "I'm really schizophrenic about this. Often I feel, if my kids don't achieve, then what have I achieved? We live in a community where everyone is trying to send their kids to great colleges, and sometimes I feel I've failed because I didn't push my kids to work that hard and they're not going to one of those schools. But then I think, my kids are happy, what does it matter? And who knows what the world will bring. This is a deep and tender area for me, and for my husband." Other parents are quite conscious of discrepancies in what they say and feel: "We tell our kids one day that we just want them to go to a college where they'll be happy, and the next day we tell them they should go to the best college they can get into." Some parents are disturbed by what they have wrought: "I realized the other day that my daughter defends people by saying they're 'smart.' Not that they're good people but that they're smart, as if being smart is the most important thing. And I had to ask myself, what did we as parents do to make her value that so much, and what's going on in our society?" Another parent said, "My daughter's role model now is Elle Woods in *Legally Blonde*—she's invested in doing well and she's ruthless. She'll work seven days a week, maybe twelve to fourteen hours a day. I would like her to have a normal life. She's really competitive. She'll say, 'I looked at *X*'s paper to see if I'm doing better, and I am, and in my head I know I'm winning.' What she's winning, I don't know. It's frightening." When it comes to talking about achievement, some parents also don't know whether honesty is, in fact, the best policy: "I don't think it's good to send double messages, but I also don't think it's right to be clear all the time—does it help my kid to say it's really important to me that you get into a great college?"

Part of what makes this achievement talk difficult is that at the root of these parents' achievement attitudes are large, conflicting cultural forces. Parents in their thirties and forties are products of a child-centered and psychological age. Some of these parents are hyperaware of the ways they have been forced to live out their parents' achievement agenda, and they're concerned about repeating that pattern with their own children. Many of these parents are preoccupied with their children's vulnerabilities and self-esteem, and fear putting too much pressure on their children. Yet at the same time many of them are dealing with deep anxiety that their children may not be able to attend the same universities that they did or enjoy the same advantages or hit the same benchmarks of achievement and success. As sociologist Arlie Hochschild puts it, "Parents are anxious about passing along to their children their own station in life. And they can't do it through land or money in a meritocracy. You do it through your kid's skills." These are quintessential American tensions.

A HEALTHY APPROACH TO ACHIEVEMENT

There is no single, healthy approach to promoting children's achievement—largely because how parents think about achievement is rooted in widely different values about money, status, and accomplishment. Yet some middle- and upper-class parents clearly need to let up on the accelerator. There are forms of achievement pressure that are reckless and unconscionable—and the pressure is not even likely to achieve what it is intended to achieve. Research indicates that children subjected to intense pressure to achieve at high levels by their parents don't outperform other students, and there's a good deal of evidence suggesting that too much focus on high achievement makes adults fragile, vulnerable to depression and anxiety. Some parents clearly need to tone down the achievement pressure while boosting their interest and engagement in other aspects of their children's lives. What seems to be especially toxic to affluent children is the combination of neglectful parenting—parents who spend little time with their kids and bail out on basic supervision—and achievement pressure. Juvenile delinquency in particular appears to spike in these circumstances. What's more, parents, like teachers, need to know particular children well enough to realize when to dial down and when to dial up achievement pressures.

Many of us as parents must become far more vigilant about the hidden messages we are sending our children about achievement, not only in the schools and communities we live in but in what consumes our time, what we admire and criticize in others, and what buoys and deflates us. Again and again I hear parents, for example, making a huge fuss about not caring where their kids go to college as long as they are happy, while asserting a clear truth—that "there are two hundred good schools and everyone has to stop focusing on just a highly selective few." But the reality is that more and more parents are trying to shoehorn their children into a small number of prestigious schools. And that hypocrisy is not lost on children. Over and over I have witnessed parents, in talking to other parents, be either visibly glum or falsely chipper—in ways that cannot possibly escape their children—as they rationalize their children attending schools that are not high status, or transparently glow when they tell other parents that their children are attending elite colleges.

So what is the healthier approach? It's crucial for parents to help their children uncover what is meaningful to them—central as that is to a strong, mature self—so that children are not just achieving to achieve or achieving to please their parents. Psychologist Charles Ducey observes that when college students who are wound up about achievement discover what's meaningful to them, the anguish around achievement often disappears. "What we find when we work with these students is that depression tends to go away when they find a passion, something that matters to them."

Children find out who they are and what's meaningful to them in part when adults are able, without an agenda, to listen in a relaxed way and to reflect back their understandings and share their knowledge of the world. Before our children's lives become jam-packed with resumé-building activities, we need to let these conversations unfold—conversations that can be wonderful for both us and our children. Some parents may also need to reckon honestly with their own fears about this conversation. As one parent at a wealthy independent high school starkly puts it: "Some of these kids don't know what they want—we've planned everything for them. And while adults around here won't admit it, I think some of them are afraid to help them figure out what they want. They want them to get with the program."

To help children find out what is meaningful to them, we as parents also need to engage in the complex choreography of leading and following—guiding children toward potentially meaningful activities and experiences and then paying careful attention to what resonates with them. We can also ask our children less about their performance at school, and more about what at school bores or engages them. We might lay the groundwork for these conversations by talking less about our accomplishments at work and more about what's engaging and interesting for us.

At the same time, it's important that we make high achievement one of a rich array of life experiences and possibilities, one among many forms of meaning and gratification and one of many ways of measuring what's valuable about oneself. This is particularly crucial because many children are not naturally academically talented or have learning difficulties, and many children will never achieve at a high level, by definition, in comparison to their peers. One way of cultivating in our children a rich and various sense of meaningfulness is for us to intentionally seek out the many forms of gratification that are unrelated to achievement and to value many kinds of life experiences. Some parents, for example, don't bombard college staff with questions only about admissions when they visit colleges with their children. They ask about many aspects of college life—the intellectual opportunities, the community spirit, the possibilities for varied friendship—and they have deep and detailed conversations with their children about these things.

HONEST SELF-REFLECTION

It will not be easy for many of us as parents to convey to our children that achievement is only one theme in the larger composition of a life, or to be vigilant about the many troubling signals that we are sending our children about achievement. It may mean wading into the muck of ourselves and coming to terms with our own feelings about achievement. Large numbers of parents have never thought about how their own views about their children's achievements are connected to the ways their parents handled achievement or about all the irrational forces that may drive them to drive their children. These forces include not only their fears of their children falling economically behind or the hope that their children will live out their dreams or compensate for their shortcomings, but their gnawing questions about their own worth in the world, their belief that their children's achievements are a clear and public reflection of their success as parents, their needling status concerns and feelings of competitiveness with other parents, and the unconscious script in their heads, written in their childhoods, that achievement is the only way to secure love—a kind of tragic condition that can be passed from generation to generation in ways and with consequences worthy of the ancient Greeks. Other parents may become myopic about achievement as a way of creating a clear direction and some sense of certainty in the face of all that is unpredictable and precarious in their child's future—high achievement is the life raft in this sea of anxiety. Still other parents, the author Alissa Quart points out, are simply terrified of their children being ordinary. "My husband thinks our son is a God and he pushes and pushes him so he'll be the world's God one day," a Chicago mother told me. In the end, some parents simply need "to grieve," as one parent put it, that their children will not accomplish in the same ways and according to the same benchmarks as they did, that they will not go to high-status colleges or land prestigious fellowships or have turbocharged careers.

This introspection is highly complicated by the fact that we have many good motives for focusing on our children's high achievements—we want them to be financially comfortable, to receive at least some recognition, to be productive members of society. It's easy for us to rationalize our achievement pressures, to convince ourselves that we are guided by these good motives, disguising from ourselves irrational ones.

But at the same time, there are moments when we can spot in ourselves deep, disturbing feelings about achievement. It should be a red flag when our self-esteem plummets when a child does poorly on a big test or is rejected by an elite independent school, when our interactions with our children are consumed by achievement talk, when we find ourselves assessing our children's competition—asking them who in their cohort gets the best grades or is applying to what colleges and checking repeatedly to see where their peers got in—or popping vocabulary flash cards at the dinner table or saying "*we* are applying" to a college or peppering college-admissions officers with questions while our children stand sullenly and idly by. It should certainly be a red flag to us when children show signs of debilitating stress as a result of academic pressure, stress that is fundamentally compromising their childhood. Psychologist and author Wendy Mogel urges parents to stick to a twenty-minute rule—spend no more than twenty minutes a day "thinking about your child's education or worrying about your child, period." Except in those cases when a child is having a significant academic or emotional problem, that's a good rule.

Finally, it may be wise for many parents to stop finessing and talk far more honestly with children about their own feelings about achievement. I am not suggesting here that we always have to tell our children the truth—children don't have to hear about all of our fleeting neurotic desires, conflicts, and irrational feelings about achievement. The parent who asks, "Does it help my kid to say it's really important to me that you get into a great college?" is not asking a dumb question. But it's hard to find a good rationale for our deceiving our older teenagers about our strong feelings about achievement. Large numbers of parents may be underestimating what a relief it would be to their children—and how much it would do to alleviate children's shame, support their maturity, and secure their respect and trust—if they stopped bobbing and weaving and surfaced these feelings, including the irrational ones.

If parents are miserable when a child does not get into a prestigious school, they might say to their child quite openly that in their more mature moments they know that's not what's important, that whether one goes to this or that college is a small part of one's life, and that their disappointment is their own problem, something they need to work on. Parents might tell their own stories about the positive and negative ways in which achievement was handled in their families of origin. These narratives help children not only understand and trust their parents more fully, but can help children spot irrational forms of achievement pressure and mitigate the shame and anger that children can feel as a result of these pressures. These narratives can also help children puzzle through how they want to be the same or different from their parents.

It's hard to know what exactly will reverse this tide of achievement pressure. It is a kind of contagion, and an escalating contagion — parents keep feeding on each other and ramping each other up. It is a collective problem that needs to be collectively addressed. It is, in a sense, a public health problem, especially given the pervasive and serious moral and emotional troubles it's creating in affluent communities. Journalist Sandra Tsing Loh suggests that college students themselves may someday soon rebel against all this pressure: "[T]his era's needed cultural statement may well be kids joyously burning *U.S. News & World Report* college rankings . . . "

But wouldn't it be better if we, as adults, took serious action first? Universities can clearly play a role by standing more strongly for many qualities of character, and by giving more weight to those qualities in admissions decisions. While some universities factor in measures of character, on a recent college tour I took with my son, most admissions officers barely talked about the kinds of moral qualities they were looking for in students. When I asked them what kinds of people they were looking for, one admissions officer simply said: "People who will advance the name of this university in the world." An admissions officer at another university said: "People who will be high impact in their field." Too many universities are dangerously catering to parents' neurotic wants and needs.

Which means that we as parents clearly have a large role as well. As parents, we have been fantastically successful at getting children to buy into our achievement ethic. It's an awesome tribute to our power as parents. But is this really the primary way we want to use our power? If we are serious about both our children's happiness and morality—and almost all parents profess to care about these things above all else—then we will have to see that we have caught a kind of fever. We can wait for children to end this contagion, or we can seek to heal ourselves.

4

WHEN BEING CLOSE TO CHILDREN BACKFIRES

AT THIS MOMENT in our history, American parents are engaged in a giant social experiment. We are seeking a new kind of closeness with our children. Legions of fathers are trying, in contrast to their own fathers, to be far more involved in their children's daily lives, attuned to their children's troubles, and open to sharing with their children their own hopes and vulnerabilities.

Because more mothers are working these days, larger numbers of fathers are taking on caretaking responsibilities—in 2002, 26 percent of husbands of employed wives cared for at least one child under age fifteen during mothers' working hours. Nine percent of fathers were the primary caregivers for these children in 2002. Conscious of how problems were buried in their own families, both mothers and fathers are seeking forms of honesty and openness in their relationships with their children—including honesty about drugs and sex—unheard of in earlier times. It appears that more parents than ever before are looking to their children for companionship—recall that middle-class parents are spending more leisure time with their children today than at almost any other time in history. One can hear parents these days, unlike previous generations of parents, brag about how close they are to their children. Some parents even brag that their children are their "best friends."

Forceful currents, to be sure, are moving in exactly the opposite direction. Staggering numbers of fathers are evaporating from their children's lives—research suggests that after several years, about a third of children born out of wedlock or whose parents divorce lose contact with their fathers; after several years, only about a quarter of these children continue to see their fathers once a week or more. Over the last roughly forty years, as women have entered the workforce in droves, many children have clearly been spending less time with their mothers. Yet even given these trends, it's clear that large numbers of parents are trying to adapt their parenting to a different age and are pioneering a way of being with children that has huge promise for their development.

Heartening as these new forms of parent-child closeness are, though, they have also brought risks to almost every aspect of children's development. Most concerning, in relying on children to fulfill basic emotional needs, many of us are inadvertently depriving children of developmental experiences that are at the heart of moral growth. To obtain maturity, appreciation for others, and ideals, children need at certain stages of development to idealize their parents—that's one powerful way in which children internalize their parents' moral qualities—and at other stages to separate from them. Yet many of us are unintentionally making it difficult for children to stay anchored to us *and* to separate in important ways—we are struggling mightily with "letting go" of our children. And many of us are making it hard for children to idealize us, in part because we are idealizing them.

The point is not to try to turn back the clock, to return to a time when it didn't occur to parents to be close to their children. But we are undertaking this great experiment without a map or a clear model in our heads. We need to understand what kinds of closeness are helpful—and harmful—to children. Why are many of us having difficulty letting go, and how can we manage these difficulties? How can we both be more involved in our children's lives, spend more relaxed, fun time with our children, *and* promote their moral and emotional growth?

THE PROBLEM

Ned Waters — a handsome, intense, somewhat guarded forty-five-year-old — grew up with three siblings outside of Hartford, Connecticut, in a family that he describes as "highly competitive" and "unemotional." While he has managed over the years to stay fairly close to one of his siblings, his relationships with the others are fragile and strained, in part because his mother always pitted them against one another. He sees his parents about once a month, yet he tends, when irritated, to snipe at them and to feel guilty afterward, or to exhaust himself containing his anger toward them. For the last ten years his relationship with his wife has been very close in some ways but troubled in others — he feels that she is almost entirely focused on taking care of both the kids and her mother, who has a chronic illness, and that he has to scrap for crumbs of attention.

His relationship with Jim, his firstborn son, was a startling contrast, a steady current of something almost indescribably sweet. "My dad didn't really know me and we didn't spend much time together, and I wanted to have a much closer relationship with Jim. And for a long time it was like we had the perfect relationship. We had a blast doing things together. I don't think I've ever had someone be so affectionate with me."

But as Jim hit adolescence, all this began to change. "In the evenings we used to read together, or he would sit on my lap and watch television. Now I get home and he's instant messaging, or playing video games with his friends, and I get the cold shoulder. It's like I'm invisible to him. I had to go on a business trip for two weeks, and I came back, and it wasn't a big hug at the door. These days I sometimes just don't want to see him at all. I can spend time with my ten-year-old, Jack, but in the back of my mind I'm thinking, when he hits adolescence he's just going to bail out on me, too. How did this happen? No one ever told me about this. This is miserable. I thought I did everything right!"

Much has been made in the last decade about parents who, hostage to their children's approval, are permissive and indulgent. Parents themselves, in our interviews, complain a great deal about this trend: "It's backboneless parenting in my neighborhood," is how one parent puts it. "Parents worry constantly about whether their kids like them." And there's good reason for concern. When parents rely too much on their children's affection and approval, they can lose their backbone; they are more apt to cater to their children's every need and to crumble in the face of their children's anger: high moral standards and effective, firm discipline go out the window. Yet this reliance on children may be corroding children's moral development in subtler yet more pervasive and damaging ways.

Many parents clearly invest deeply in their children and feel a deep harmony, a symbiotic bond with their children during their child's infancy and early childhood. For others, like Ned, this time is preadolescence, when their children are around seven to twelve years old—a stage when their children are easy, fun, adoring companions.

These close relationships are often simply wonderful for both children and parents. Some parents, like Ned, who have had troubled, fractured relationships with their own parents and siblings, can find in this symbiotic closeness exactly what they have always craved: another human being who gives them undivided attention, who envelops them with affection, who overlooks or easily forgives their flaws. It would be hard, in fact, to overstate the profound sense of completeness—the feeling that the world is finally in joint, set right—that some parents experience for the first time when they have this uncritical, unequivocal love. It's no wonder that many of these parents come to idealize their children and their relationships with them—an idealization that can become crucial to the parents' security and sense of wholeness.

Yet for children this idealization can be another story, imperiling their steps toward healthy independence and moral functioning. Adolescents come into their own and develop key moral qualities in part by testing how their parents view them and how they know themselves against how they are known by various other children and adults. The world becomes a kind of laboratory, as Erik Erikson observes, in which they repeatedly categorize and recategorize themselves. A teenager might, for example, float among different cliques, or attach herself to multiple mentors, keenly attentive to whether a relationship brings out her "truest" self. Over time, healthy adolescents arrive at a self-definition or a sense of self that consolidates both old and new roles, that integrates their parents' moral expectations and standards, and that expresses some sense of who they feel they are at their core. (Identity is not—as is often popularly believed—then locked in. But there is more organization and a greater sense of unity in the adult self. Although adults may also have multiple self-representations, may feel that they are different people in different situations and may go through changes in identity, adults develop a kind of narrative, a story about themselves, that organizes these different notions of self.)

It is this coherent, distinct sense of self that is at the core of morality in adulthood. It enables young people as they enter adulthood to appreciate others as independent and distinct, to engage in mature, reciprocal relationships with other adults, including their parents, to give to others authentically, and to take responsibility for others over time.

Unhealthy separations, in contrast, can undermine moral growth in various ways. Burdened by their parents' needs, some children seek to disconnect themselves from their parents and rely too much on their peers' standards and expectations. Some children struggle with feelings of obligation to parents that seem foreign and imposed, or children get stuck in the nest, hindering their capacity for healthy, caring relationships. I remember as a therapist seeing a fourteen-year-old girl, still tightly caught in her parents' orbit and anxious to please them, who struggled to connect to her peers. She expected other children to quickly tune in to her needs, as her parents did, and was uncomfortable with normal adolescent teasing—her parents frowned upon teasing. She became increasingly less popular and started to be the brunt of her peers' jokes. She responded by becoming highly moralistic and superior with them—by becoming too adult—only distancing them further.

For children to separate in healthy ways, then, parents need to separate as well. Our challenge is to relinquish the gratification and power of influencing many aspects of how children view themselves and the narcissistic satisfaction of being the center of our children's world. While we need to continue to assert high moral expectations, we also need to recede to the edge of our children's consciousness—even to endure temporarily feeling like nobody, being "invisible" to our child—while we enable a child's peers and other adults to influence our children's self-definitions and to become the focus of their lives. What can be hardest for us is giving up this influence even when our children seem to be becoming foreign to us or different from what we had hoped. As research psychologist Donna Wick observes, often parents also feel they have been their "best selves"—generous, loving, flexible—in their relationships with their children, and they must painfully relinquish these gratifying self-images as their children become teenagers.

For entirely healthy parents, even in the best circumstances, these separations in adolescents are rarely simple. Many parents dealing with separation can feel unceremoniously booted out of Nirvana, ripped from a kind of womb. Psychologists now talk about parents' struggles to "grieve" the separations of their adolescents. A Boston psychiatrist half-jokingly says that parents' these days suffer from "letting go disorder." Often parents feel some mixture of rejected, unappreciated, inadequate. Some parents, like Ned, feel blind-sided: "No one ever told me about this!" As one of our interviewees, a thoughtful fiftyish mother said to me. "I'm very close to my husband. But I am closer to my daughter. I've never had an easier, less ambivalent relationship. And then it seemed that she just turned on me when she hit about thirteen. And it was just terrible. It was a huge loss and I didn't see it coming. It was the most painful thing I've ever experienced."

For most parents these feelings around separation are temporary and contained and unharmful to their children. Yet it can be another story when children are idealized or are their parents' "best friends," or when parents like Ned are looking to these relationships to fill holes in their other primary relationships or to heal old childhood fractures.

In these circumstances, parents are far more likely to regress, to recoil, and to feel disillusioned — "I did everything right!" Ned protests. In a fog of anger and hurt, some parents lose their capacity to take their children's perspectives or to see who their children have become. "When my son began to separate from me, I became so caught up with myself it was like a wall came up and I couldn't see him on the other side of it" is how one parent put it. To avoid further aggravating the relationship, these wounded parents may pull back on their moral expectations. "When my son started to separate, I started to pick my fights, because I didn't want to further jeopardize the relationship," a mother tells me. "It drove me crazy that he wasn't nicer with my friends, but I was reluctant to put that demand on him. In retrospect, I think I should have." Other wounded parents overreact to the provocations and daily irritations, the million paper cuts an adolescent can inflict. These parents are quick to anger or, like Ned, to withdraw. Either way, children are deprived of a secure base and of access to parents' moral guidance. I have talked to fathers, like Ned, who are dealing with particular, tough feelings that may hamper separation. They have tried to be closer to their children than their fathers were to them and they feel, when their children hit adolescence, that they have failed at this critical life project. They may also have no internal images or models — based on images of their own fathers — of letting go.

Still other parents unknowingly squash their children's independence by micromanaging—the infamous "helicopter" parents, hovering and swooping in regularly to avert distress—and tightly controlling children's leisure time. A small fraction of parents are going to great lengths to head off these separations. A new initiative, the Mother-Daughter Project, invites mothers to attend workshops with their daughters beginning at age seven to anticipate later strains in the mother-daughter relationship and to avoid their daughters' rebellions.

Parents can similarly struggle at developmental stages earlier than adolescence when their children become more independent, again compromising the separations vital to moral growth. Research psychologist Wick describes a mother who can't bear her infant's separations—this mother describes being jealous of babysitters and both "hating it" when her infant "melts down" when she's not there and "loving it" because it signals her infant's dependence on her. As children enter elementary school, some parents struggle with separation, and summer camp isn't what it used to be: some parents are not only in constant e-mail contact but give their children web cameras and regularly survey their activities, sneak their children cell phones in violation of camp policies, and constantly badger camp staff to gather information about their kids.

And these days these problems with separation don't end in adolescence. Much has been made in recent years about how many college students and young people remain destructively dependent on their parents.

Nearly 50 percent of the class of 2007 said they planned to move home for at least a little while postcollege, and 80 percent of eighteen- to twenty-five-year-olds say they have talked to their parents in the past day, an astonishing change in the experience of young adulthood. I am not simply joining the pundits who love to lampoon coddled twenty-somethings. Many young people after college are living with their parents because they simply can't financially survive on their own in our economy, and many young adults, during a time when they can feel dangerously disconnected and at sea, can greatly benefit from being anchored to parents. It's also wrong to view young people's desire to remain strongly and immediately connected during college as pathological. In many other countries young people don't typically separate at college, and most young people are perfectly capable of both having strong and deep relationships with their parents during college and separating significantly.

But in some cases young people can't separate because they have been infantilized by their parents from early ages and simply can't function on their own. Research by psychologist Jerome Kagan reveals how anxious, smothering parenting in the first years of life can make children fragile, depressed, and easily influenced by others. Some college staff now worry that students, abetted by technology, are far too involved with their parents in ways that are both a cause and a reflection of this deep dependence, that parents are doing everything but planting a wire in their children when they leave for college. "My son never calls!" a parent recently bemoaned to me. "I only talk to him every other day." Some parents seek to have their hands in almost every aspect of their children's college experience. On a recent college visit with my son, while touring a dorm, one parent asked how many stalls there were in the bathroom, another asked if there was a rotating shower schedule, and a third asked "whether the washing machines take coins or cards." "I wish my parents had some hobby other than me," a young person told psychologist David Anderegg. College deans and counselors have come up with names for dependent, fragile students who unravel away from home—"teacups" and "krispies."

There are several parenting stances and guidelines, as I take up later in this chapter, that can help us as parents create healthy boundaries with our children. I want to highlight just a few here. While it's important for us to establish rituals that enable us to have regular and meaningful contact with our children—research points to the value of regular family dinners, for example—outside of these rituals it's crucial to give children choice in deciding when and how much to be with us. "One piece of advice that I give myself and that I find reassuring is just to follow my child's cues," a mother and parent educator from Cleveland says. "There are times when my son calls from college frequently and times when he hardly ever calls, and it's largely a reflection of his needs. But that's his way of working toward independence, and if I can trust and follow him, I think he'll achieve a healthy independence."

We can also regularly ask ourselves whether we might unknowingly be creating unhealthy dependence. The mother who recognizes that she is threatened by the babysitter's closeness to her infant is demonstrating important self-awareness. As children separate, we can, too, work to hold in our heads the simple truth that a child's desire for separation is a sign of a strong, unconflicted child-parent relationship, not a sign of a fraught, troubled one, that what we experience as a loss of closeness our children may not be experiencing at all and that children may measure closeness in ways that are different from us. While at times I see parents beam with delight about how often they talk to their kids or unhappy about how infrequently they converse, the frequency of these conversations, as the mother above suggests, is no real barometer of closeness—infrequent contact is just as likely to be a sign of healthy, secure closeness as frequent contact.

THE IMPORTANCE OF IDEALIZATION

A couple of years ago I was on a plane to Chicago. I began talking to a man about my age sitting beside me. Our conversation turned to our kids. Kind and lighthearted, he remarked on how much he valued his close relationship with his seventeen-year-old son, and we both talked about how different this closeness was from our relationships with our fathers.

But then he said something jolting. Suddenly I realized that we were not, in fact, talking about the same kind of closeness at all: "I just really enjoy hanging out with my son and his friends. It's like we're all equal, like there's no real difference between me and them. We have a great time together."

When we as parents become too dependent on our children for closeness, it can undercut another process crucial to moral development—idealization. Most children naturally idealize their parents throughout childhood and sometimes through adolescence —they see their parents as calm, infallible, omnipotent—and this idealization is one powerful way in which children develop maturity and internalize values and ideals. As the legendary psychoanalyst Heinz Kohut observed, the self develops not only through the mirroring of adults but through internalizing the confident expectations, values, and ideals of adults who are temporarily put on a pedestal.

Parents who idealize their children or who want to be their children's friends can disrupt the process of idealization in several ways. It's clearly much harder for children to idealize us when we engage them as "equals," as the father above does, or when we fail to represent our authority. Children have no incentive to become like us—because the message we're giving is that they already are—and the world can simply be frightening to children who don't think we have more moral wisdom or authority than they do.

Children also don't naturally idealize us when they frequently feel that they need to take care of us or deal with our vulnerabilities, and large numbers of children are treated by parents like siblings or as partners from young ages. Children are asked to co-parent siblings or even, in certain respects, to parent their parents in many kinds of households, whether poor, single-parent homes where mothers are highly stressed or wealthy homes where parents are emotionally fragile.

Another group of parents—parents who are constantly hovering and micromanaging—can also make it hard for children to idealize them. It's hard for children to respect parents who both constantly serve them and express so little confidence or trust in them. Further, children need to internalize us, to make our admired moral skills and attributes their own, yet micromanaging parents give their children little occasion or reason to internalize them. Children need to experience what Kohut calls "optimal frustration"—they have to experience us at times as failing to meet their needs—so that they have both the opportunity and the motivation to learn how to function independently and to adopt our admired traits.

THE CLOSENESS DILEMMA

"It's much muddier for me than it was for my parents," Sylvia, a parent from San Francisco, tells me. "They were very clear that they were the parent and that parenting was not a dialogue. It was about teaching me certain things. I want to be much closer to my daughter, I want to know what's going on in her life, and I want her to be able to tell me what she's thinking and feeling. But I also know that I'm the adult and that I should expect to be treated as an adult. I want Debbie to tell me when I'm irritating her, but then when she says to me—'Mom, you're being an idiot'—I say to myself, 'I would never have talked to my parents that way.' Figuring this out is the hardest thing I've ever done."

While some parents are unaware of the ways in which closeness is damaging to their children, many of us are quite consciously struggling with real dilemmas—dilemmas that have significant implications for our children's moral development—that are directly created by our closeness to them. Some parents, like Sylvia, find themselves, for example, ricocheting senselessly between being authority figures and being friends. They want their children to be relaxed and comfortable with them and to feel empowered to criticize them, for instance, or they want to engage in the kinds of rough banter with their teens that their teens engage in with their friends. But in the face of this banter or this criticism they sometimes feel that a line has been crossed—a line that often seems random and mysterious to their children—and that their own authority has been breached. I certainly have had this experience. One minute I will bond with my own children about some dumb comment a teacher made, and the next minute I'll be emphasizing how important it is for them to respect their teacher, a kind of reversal that can be confusing and seem hypocritical to them, as they don't hesitate to tell me.

Other parents who have close relationships with their children simply find themselves in over their heads, confronting complex moral dilemmas that they don't know how to resolve, often around confidentiality. Thirteen-year-old Owen, for example, says to his mother that he is going to tell her something confidentially and then reports that he is concerned about his friend John, who is getting stoned after school almost every day. But, he tells his mom, if she tells John's parents or teacher, he will end up a pariah at his school. Because she is a trusted confidante, his mother must think hard before calling John's parents—she must figure out how to both help John and prevent Owen from being ostracized. Shira's parents are close to her and to her friends, and one of Shira's friends reveals confidentially that she is depressed and won't talk to her parents anymore—Shira's parents have to figure out whether and how to intervene. Maria admits to her father that she lied to him about where she was on a Saturday night—she didn't want him to know that she was at a party where there was drinking—but her father can't decide whether to punish her or applaud her honesty. He prides himself on being close to his daughter and has told her that he values honesty in the relationship above all else.

Parents' closeness with their children may be endangering their moral development in two additional ways. Another parent we spoke with was quite conscious that "because I understand [my child] so well and know why he does what he does" she sometimes excuses behavior that should be punished. Some parents' intoxication with their closeness with their kids may also be causing them to overestimate how well they know their children and can trust their judgment, causing them to ignore developmental risks—they don't require their teenagers to tell them where they are, they let their teens stay out too late, they do nothing to protect their children from their children's friends who may pose risks. Parents are not thinking clearly, for example, when they leave their kids home alone for the weekend because, as one suburban parent told journalist Melissa Ludtke, "We are trying to show the kids how much we trust them."

HEALTHY CLOSENESS WITH CHILDREN

There are no easy solutions to these parenting challenges and conundrums. Even in the best circumstances, many of us as parents are trying to take on what seems at times to be contradictory tasks. We are trying to communicate responsibility for others yet still be a confidant, to be vulnerable and honest about our flaws yet still be worthy of necessary idealization, to respect our children's judgment and freedom yet know when to assert authority or command deference, to have warm, close relationships with our children that fulfill important needs for us but that are elastic, that bear separation and launch children into the wider world.

While there is no formula or script for being this parent, there are certain guideposts.

We can, for one, seek to get beyond platitudes about either being close to children or being traditional authority figures, as if these are the only two possible parenting stances. Far better to have conversations with each other that help us know, based on the context, when to engage a child's views and when to insist on deference, when to tell a child that we can't keep a confidence, how and when to reveal our flaws, when and how to be intimate, and when and how to assert our authority. To understand how and when to assert our authority, it will help us to understand, for example, how children in a particular situation experience their relationship with us. When Sylvia's child calls her an "idiot," it's important for Sylvia not to evaluate the comment in terms of what it would have meant in her relationship with her own mother, but to understand what the specific meaning of this comment is in terms of the history of her relationship with her daughter. Is it a way of being close or an act of disrespect? To determine whether we should call the parent of our child's friend who is getting stoned every day, we should work to gather more information and to weigh many factors—What will it mean to our child if we break a confidence? Will breaking this confidence cause our child to shut us out completely, eliminating the chance that we will be told when someone else is in more serious danger? Is the parent we might call likely to respond constructively or destructively? While some action is necessary, might it be more productive to call a school counselor or to engage some other adult who is better positioned to engage this family? Will the school counselor protect our child's confidentiality?

What may be most important, though, is for us to understand that we are undergoing pivotal developmental experiences along with our children, and to develop wisdom about how to meet these developmental challenges and tasks. While psychologists have studied carefully how children idealize and gradually de-idealize their parents, there's little literature or wisdom on parents' idealizing their children or on working through the loss of this idealization, a particular kind of disillusionment. While we fuss a great deal about whether children are constructively separating from their parents, we rarely think about whether parents are positively separating from their children, let alone about how to guide parents in these separations.

While research is needed, here especially it is important that we recognize that we are not playing an automatic role or simply being role models, but enduring losses that are likely to stir up all sorts of old longings and wounds. It's important, too, for us to see that taking vacations without our kids or sending them to camp may not only be key to developing their independence but also to developing our own, so that we can work to master the anxieties and vulnerabilities created by these separations. It may also help for us to focus specifically on our relationships with our own parents—on how we may be looking to our children for some kind of emotional sustenance that our parents failed to provide and on what patterns we may be unwittingly repeating with our children. I recently spoke with a mother, Pam, whose introspection and understanding of her own relationship with her parents helped her facilitate her five-year-old daughter's healthy separation. Pam was angry at her daughter for being "sassy." But, as she put it, "My anger was somehow bigger than my daughter's behavior—I got so mad at the way she was so brazen with me sometimes. And I realized what I was angry about . . . I had a lot of sadness and anger about my daughter growing up and becoming more independent and entitled—in a good way—to life than I ever was . . . My mother had a hard time with my being independent. I realized that my daughter's independence, ironically, might be the result of my being a better parent than my mother was. And when I realized that, I felt a lot more compassion for my daughter and more confident as a mother." It is also useful for us to be mindful of how our close relationships with our children might be diminishing or fraying our ties to other adults we hold dear and who might help us as parents. One major survey suggests that American parents today have fewer confidants than parents twenty years ago.

Whether or not we succeed or fail in this giant social experiment in closeness will have reverberations for many generations to come. As parents we always need to ask ourselves: What will the next generation of parents seek to embrace and change about our parenting? Will these parents want to reproduce the kinds of closeness we have sought with our kids in their own relationships with their children? Or will they view that closeness as a problem to be corrected, or even as dangerously naive, and seek a cleaner authority role and a brighter line separating them and their children?

The answer clearly depends on how we manage our closeness with our children. My hope is that we will never return to a time when it doesn't occur to parents to be close to their children, a time when parenting was viewed less as a layered, deep relationship and more as a set of tasks, however those tasks were defined. The benefits to children of more emotionally available and present parents are too great. But we should seek this closeness only if we are willing to shoulder the hard responsibility for it, the careful and intense self-searching, the anguishing moments of separation and loss, the stretches of ambiguity, the deliberate, relentless parsing of what we are doing for our children's sake and what we are doing for our own.

5

MORAL ADULTS: MORAL CHILDREN

IN THE BROTHERS GRIMM fairy tale "The Old Grandfather and the Grandson," a young married couple has grown tired of the husband's father, who lives with them, and who has become increasingly feeble. They stop inviting him to the dinner table and begin feeding him small portions from a dishpan.

One day they watch their small son gathering some bits of wood on the ground; he is building something. "What are you doing there?" asks the father. Misha says, "Dear father, I am making a dishpan. So that when you and dear Mother become old, you may be fed from this dishpan."

The husband and wife look at one another and, ashamed, begin to weep. From then on they seat the grandfather at the table and wait on him.

"In the hours after my first child was born, I got to sit with him by myself for a while," says fifty-three-year-old James. "And something profound happened. I used to have a pretty terrible self-image. I was self-centered, and I knew it, and I didn't like it. But at that moment I had such love for him, and I felt that I had so much to give to him. I realized that I had been given a phenomenal gift. It suddenly came to me that I didn't have to be selfish anymore. I could be a different person and it could start with my being self-less in relation to him. And this wasn't just some powerful moment that quickly passed. My kids are now in college, and I am a much better person now."

Americans have great faith in their capacity to improve their well-being. As many as 40 percent of Americans in the early 1990s belonged to self-help or support groups of some kind, and bookstores are rife with bold tomes empowering adults to tame fears, dispatch obsessions, and deal with people they can't stand (the book I'm dying to read is *Emotional Healing at Warp Speed*). When it comes to ridding ourselves of painful flaws, and mood improvement, our faith in the plasticity of personality appears to be endless.

Yet most of us don't even have in our heads a concept that is far more important to our children, our society, and ultimately to our own well-being: the possibility of our own moral growth. Most of us believe that at some point in childhood our moral qualities are essentially locked in. While we might push ourselves to be more honest and generous in specific situations, we see our moral character as largely, if not entirely, set in stone.

Many adults, to be sure, change very little in the course of adulthood. There are narcissistic adults who never develop any real capacity to understand others, and there are adults whose compassion and integrity remain steady and deep throughout life. But to imagine moral character as unchanging is to grossly misunderstand the nature of most adults' lives.

For the reality, according to fresh research, is that our moral qualities as adults can vacillate depending on many factors, with large consequences for our children's moral development. While many of us lose our ideals over time, others of us do not develop serious ideals until well into midlife. Some adults become wiser, more able to discern important moral truths; others' notions of fairness become more formulaic and coarse. Some adults become more selfish while others become more altruistic—new research shows that the elderly, contrary to popular belief, tend to become more other-centered. (King Lear does not develop any real feeling for others until he nears death.) While Americans these days worship young people who are often selfish, and obsess about the losses that come with aging, it is often not until well into adulthood that we tend to develop our most important qualities, including empathy for many kinds of people leading many kinds of lives, the capacity to love others despite their flaws, the ability to shield others from our destructive qualities. Based on his studies of adult lives, psychologist Gil Noam questions the whole notion of moral maturity. Every stage of adulthood, Noam argues, creates new vulnerability to regression, disintegration, and character rigidity, as well as new strengths. Sometimes adults undergo entire self-reorganizations—and sometimes these changes greatly impact their ability to cultivate children's moral qualities. When children become self-absorbed and impulsive in their teen years, it is widely recognized as a sea change—we view adolescence as a restructuring of the personality, a reorganization of the self. Yet when adults in midlife become self-absorbed and impulsive, we call it "a crisis" or say they have "issues." Some of these adults, though, are in fact developing fundamentally different self-understandings and sources of meaning that radically reorder their relationships and boost or corrode their ability to parent or mentor.

Perhaps nothing tests adults and shapes adult development more than the experience of parenting. We as parents don't influence children in a simple, linear way: we are engaged in complex relationships with children—and enmeshed in complex family dynamics—that constantly affect how we respond to children. Adults and children powerfully affect one another's emotional and moral development. That's true even in infancy. Depression researchers at Boston Medical Center have observed a common destructive cycle, for example, between depressed mothers and low-birthweight babies, who tend to be less responsive to their caregivers: these babies' lethargy causes their mothers to withdraw further, which causes the babies to reach out to their mothers even less, which in turn causes their mothers to become less responsive—a downward spiral that can imperil the development of empathy in infants. Some of us as parents also regress in our relationship with our children because of emotional troubles, such as depression, or because we find ourselves repeating old, destructive relationship patterns—patterns that have deep roots in our own childhoods. Sometimes these relationships spiral downward as a parent's own developmental stage destructively interacts with a child's developmental needs. One reason that relationships between adults and teenagers can become so toxic is that adults can be caught up in the intense self-concerns of a midlife crisis at exactly the same time that their children are caught up in the intense self-concerns of adolescence.

Yet, in the course of parenting, other parents such as James discover for the first time powerful capacities for empathy, sacrifice, and moral awareness. In all sorts of ways, parenting can lift parents' moral blinders. Parents may learn to deal with their selfish qualities or defects because they see the damage they cause to their children, or because they see these qualities reflected in their children's qualities or actions—as Misha's parents do in the Brothers Grimm fairy tale—or as they come to admire qualities in their children that they lack.

Perhaps most important, parenting requires us to focus deeply on another human being, often for the first time. In the face of that challenge, some adults, like James, develop much stronger capacities to appreciate others and to love—there are, in fact, many stages of perspective-taking and appreciation through which parents can progress.

As parents and mentors, it's vital to see ourselves not as static role models but as imperfect human beings, continually developing, in our dynamic relationships with our children, our own moral and mentoring capacities. The subtleties of appreciating and being generous with others, acting with fairness and integrity, and formulating mature and resilient ideals are a life's work: "There is nothing noble in being superior to someone else," the civil rights leader Whitney Young said. "The only real nobility is in being superior to your former self."

What causes changes in our moral qualities? What are the obstacles to our becoming more effective parents and moral mentors, and how can these obstacles be overcome? How can we foster our own moral growth?

SEEING — AND NOT SEEING — OUR CHILDREN

It is late afternoon and I am in a small room entombed in fluorescent light. I am conducting a focus group with eight women — most are repeat drug offenders — in a minimum-security correctional facility. I am trying to help a local organization think through what kinds of supports or programs might be useful for children at high risk of juvenile delinquency. We want to hear from these women what they think will be most beneficial to their children.

A couple of the women express only disappointment and frustration with their children. One woman in particular, Diane, seems to ooze contempt for her ungrateful daughter: "She just thinks about herself." A few other women are quite candid about how ashamed they are for failing their children. One recommends that a program offering the support and guidance of stable adult figures, especially men, be created for their daughters.

Two of the women seem to have used their time in prison to reflect a great deal about their relationships with their children and about how they could be most effective as parents. June, who grew up in rural Georgia, is focused on avoiding the mistakes of her own mother. "I hear a lot about promoting self-esteem, but that's not what I learned as a child. I was beaten as a child and I was seen but not heard, so sometimes it's hard for me to parent another way. But I know it's critical for my child to be heard. I try to treat every word she says as important, as vibrantly important." Leslie — wiry, pretty, pale, intense — goes further: "I know my daughter doesn't trust me, and I don't blame her. Three times I told her that I would stop abusing drugs and every time I went back. She could use a mentor. But mostly I think she needs a group, or some place, where she can talk about how many times I've abandoned her and how angry she is at me. She needs to talk about how much she hates me."

While adults can evolve in many ways, there are a few forms of adult development that are most critical in shaping children's moral development. Over time, we as parents and mentors not only have to develop a stronger capacity to take children's perspective, we have to understand specifically how children perceive us, including whether and in what ways they trust and respect us. Effective parents or mentors, as I suggested earlier, also appreciate what is particular about a child, and they are able to recognize key developmental changes and transformations in a child's character: These parents and mentors hold a story of a child that is fluid, evolving. Valuing something particular in a child may sound obvious or easy—we talk a great deal about recognizing what is unique in a child—yet even the best parents can struggle to know and value a child who is unlike them or who does not fulfill their hopes or fit one of their story lines. I am thinking here of a mother I spoke with who was a tomboy, and who works to summon enthusiasm for the vanities of her highly feminine, fashion-diva daughter; of an intellectual father who can't easily fathom his child's sports interests and desire to have a business career; of a father, who is not spiritual, who has difficulties connecting to his daughters' constant barrage of questions about death and God; and of a risk-averse mother finally figuring out that her fiercely adventurous daughter thrives on risk.

At the same time, it helps a great deal if we as parents and mentors can step outside the relationship, taking a more objective, helicopter view—and ask ourselves how our ideal self, or a respected third person, would handle a troubling situation with a child. I sometimes think about what my wife would do, or what a friend of mine who is a superb father would do, when I find myself knotted up about an issue with my own children. That's how we can both bring our highest standards and wisdom to a relationship and act in our children's interests even when it conflicts with our own wants and needs. Finally, as psychologist Robert Selman's work on perspective-taking suggests, it helps us to understand something about the history of our relationship with a child, as well as how our own context and history—including our own experience as a child—can both inform and misinform our understanding of our child's needs, history, and life.

Parents have greatly varying capacities to engage in these various forms and levels of perspective-taking. Some parents, like Diane, have virtually no capacity to take their children's perspectives or to separate those points of view from their own. A few of the women in the correctional facility knew that their children could benefit from a mentor, but they could not seem to focus on how their children perceived them as mentors, on the more specific needs of their children, on what would help repair their relationships with their children, or—with the exception of June—on how their own history might affect their parenting. Leslie, on the other hand, not only recognizes how she is perceived by her daughter, she is able to step outside the relationship and assess what's best for her daughter and for the relationship. The line between her daughter's needs and her own is so clear to her that she is able to take her daughter's perspective and act in her daughter's interest even at a cost to herself, even if it means her daughter fully realizing her intense anger toward her. Leslie also sees the relationship historically—she recognizes a long-standing pattern in her relationship with her daughter—and she brings to the relationship high standards: she understands the importance of her daughter holding her to a high standard.

WHAT CAUSES MORAL GROWTH AND REGRESSION

These capacities for perspective-taking, as Selman observes, ᷍ not fixed—they vary by situation and they can change throug' adult life. While these changes are caused by many factors, two things may be most central. Certain moods, especially anxiety and depression, can undermine one's capacity for perspective-taking. Twenty percent of adults will suffer a major depression at some point in adulthood, an agonizing, isolating illness—chronicled in popular books such as William Styron's *Darkness Visible*—which typically includes intense feelings of worthlessness, anger, and despair; and large numbers of parents will suffer low-level depression for long periods, often a steady drizzle of helplessness and hopelessness.

It would be terribly unfair to ignore that many of these parents, despite these moods, are wonderful parents—and parenting well in the face of depression often requires no small amount of pluck and courage. Yet depression can be intensely self-absorbing and diminish parents' ability to listen, empathize, or carry with them a third-person perspective, impairments that parents are sometimes painfully aware of: "My daughter is feisty and strong-willed, and when I'm not depressed it's a quality I love about her," a lovely, generous mother who suffers from serious bouts of depression told me. "But when I'm depressed I can't bear it. The last time I was depressed I said to her: 'I don't want to be your mother anymore.' I was the wicked witch." Not surprisingly, the costs of parental depression to children's emotional and moral growth can be large. Children of depressed parents are far more likely to abuse drugs, to become depressed themselves, and to suffer behavior problems than are children with nondepressed parents. I'll have more to say about depression later.

GHOSTS IN THE NURSERY

Parents' capacities for perspective-taking are perhaps more commonly undercut by another powerful factor. Parents unknowingly re-create old, destructive relationship patterns in their interactions with their children. In the 1970s, the renowned psychoanalyst Selma Fraiberg wrote of the many unseen ways parents' reflexes with their children are shaped by their own relationships with their parents. Fraiberg spoke of "ghosts in the nursery"—"visitors from the unremembered pasts of the parents, uninvited guests at the christening." Early in our lives we develop basic attachment patterns, understandings about what a relationship is and basic ways of relating in our interactions with our parents. These patterns are reproduced and reworked in subsequent relationships, including, often most profoundly, in our relationships with our own children.

Often this reworking is perfectly healthy. Yet especially when parents feel vulnerable, neglected, or out of control in their relationships with their children, they are apt to revert back to old, familiar ways of being—behaviors that they thought they had permanently shed or outgrown—no matter how unsuccessful those ways of being were in the past. As parents deal more primitively with their children, their children often respond primitively to them, and this response often further fragments parents' abilities to interpret their children's experience, to step outside the relationship and to deal with their child constructively.

Take Rita, an affable, bright single mother, and her seventeen-year-old son Wayne, who shares his mother's sweet, engaging quality. I have known Rita and Wayne for many years, and prior to his adolescence, both Wayne and Rita described their relationship as close. Wayne had always been protective of Rita, including rigorously screening her suitors. But around the time Wayne turned fourteen, all this began to change. Wayne began staying out too late, skipping school, ignoring his mother's simple requests, treating her as if she was stupid. I know from Wayne that he was hurt both by his mother's almost daily criticism of him and by her focus on his younger sister, who was struggling in school. Yet to Rita, Wayne's was the worst kind of male arrogance. "He's like too many men I have known," Rita tells me. "He's like my father, my old boyfriends, my former husband. I heard the way he talked to a girl on the phone the other day, like she was trash. I can't bear it." Enraged at Wayne, Rita utterly lost her capacity to understand his perspective and began to deal with him more and more imperiously, which only exacerbated Wayne's contempt. One day when I was at their house Wayne arrived and Rita bombarded him with a long list of complaints, all pointing to his selfishness and negligence. He gave her the finger. Her response to him was swift: "Get the hell out of my house."

While Rita's deep anger was fueled by her damaging history with men, this kind of regression can take many forms and can occur at many stages in parents' lives. Some parents, for example, subjected to unwanted intrusions or unpredictable attacks as children — whether from a volatile parent, from a parent who sought their attention inappropriately, or from a highly abusive older sibling — become rigid and controlling in their primary relationships. These parents may be swamped by old angers and vulnerabilities that blind them to their children's perspectives and cause them to lash out destructively when either a toddler or a teenager is, say, moody and antagonistic.

And old angers and vulnerabilities can undermine parents as moral mentors in many other ways. Previous vulnerabilities and ways of relating are often at work when a parent finds herself frightened of disciplining a child because she fears that her child will stop caring about her, or stifling a child's steps toward independence because she fears her child will abandon her. While some parents regress in the face of their children's separations and rebellions, other parents find themselves regressing in the face of their children's dependence. When I was a therapist, I saw a father who kept shaming his five-year-old daughter for being needy and demanding because he failed to recognize the real issue — he could not bear her dependence on him — which only made her more fragile and dependent.

Depression and anxiety can also undermine parents' moral and mentoring abilities in many ways. Over the last several years I have talked with several older children and young adults who had grown up with depressed parents. A few of these children spoke of hostility and criticism that was constant, withering, unprovoked, of "needing to walk on eggshells," of their parents' Jekyll-and-Hyde mood swings. Sheila, a Boston parent, admits that before entering a family support program, when she felt helpless and overwhelmed she would hit and scream at her children "because they were the only things in my life I could control." Some children feel great shame—believing they deserve their parents' carping or even caused their parents' depression. "Depressed parents are usually too ashamed of their depression to talk about it," observes child psychiatrist William Beardslee, a pioneering depression researcher. "Children develop theories about why it's undiscussed, theories that are most often egocentric and self-blaming."

ADULTS' GREAT POTENTIAL FOR MORAL GROWTH

Yet there is another side to this story. Vulnerabilities and bumps in the road can spur in parents, like the parents in the Brothers Grimm story, deeper moral capacities and new, more constructive parenting approaches. Self-aware adults who are committed to their own moral growth can, in fact, seize many different kinds of opportunities to more clearly see their children's perspectives, to curb their destructive behaviors, and to acquire important moral capacities and understandings in their relationships with their children.

Research psychologist Donna Wick describes the mother who assumes her infant can't bear her absences—because she suffered incapacitating separation anxiety as a child and couldn't bear her own mother's temporary departures. This mother comes to understand how her needs in her relationship with her infant are driven by vulnerabilities connected to the way she was parented, enabling her to become less selfish. This mother recognizes both that she is conflating her and her daughter's needs and that this conflation is self-serving; it's a way of keeping her daughter close, of keeping her from separating.

Sometimes adults and children can scaffold each other's moral strengths. Anne Layton, a Boston mother, becomes committed to standing up for herself more effectively—and guiding her daughter in developing this quality—as she witnesses her daughter become increasingly hesitant in voicing her views.

Some adults describe explicitly how they learn from children themselves—they don't simply see children as empty cans into which they can deposit their wisdom. They allow children to mentor them in key respects. Ken Winners, a Detroit father, tells me that he thinks he's learned more from his son than his son has learned from him about empathizing with other people. Regina Jones, an elementary school teacher, feels that a ten-year-old boy in her classroom is better able to take other children's perspectives and to work out conflicts than she is: she says she is trying to learn from him how to create a classroom that is more fair. Mike Ryan, a white basketball coach, thinks that certain white kids on his team have greater understanding and relate more easily to black players than he does—he is trying to learn from them. In the course of parenting, Maria learns from her daughter to stand by what's true and right even if others don't approve. "My daughter got into trouble in school and I worried about what other people thought, and she had the maturity to say to me, 'I've got to think about what I did and sort out whether it was right or wrong and forget about what other people think.' She didn't want to be a tumbleweed. And that was coming from an adolescent. It got me thinking about how dependent I am on what other people think and it helped me begin to get over it."

Other parents' moral standards are bolstered as they become more mindful of what they are modeling for their children: "Once you become a parent you start to think harder about the kind of citizen you are," a parent from a Chicago suburb says. "Just recently, my wife and I had to fill out a form stating how many hours our son had driven with us—you need a certain number of hours to get a driver's license. We could have fudged it—I've fudged this kind of thing before. But then we thought: This is a good law, and what kind of message would fudging send to our son about what it means to be a responsible citizen or community member?"

Still other parents experience a deepened sense of humanity in the course of parenting: "When my daughter was born, I felt a deep and unequivocal love for her that was like nothing I'd ever experienced," a Chicago father tells me. "And that love extended out. You can see the world in a different light, feel connected to others in a different way. You feel a deeper love for other people." Another parent felt greater connection in another sense. "When I had kids, I started to feel this tie to anyone who has been a parent, to parents from other cultures and communities. You start to see every kid as your kid, every parent's dilemma as your dilemma, that there's a universal experience and language."

TAKING CHARGE OF OUR OWN MORAL DEVELOPMENT

There is no single strategy, of course, that will stop us as parents from regressing. There's no magic elixir that will help us realize our moral potential. Yet there is much that we can do on both counts.

We can, for one, work to manage depression and other destructive moods. That will mean, if we spot in ourselves symptoms of depression, overcoming the inner and outer roadblocks to getting treatment—both for our own and for our children's sake. Hopelessness is, for example, both a cause and a consequence of depression and a major obstacle to getting treatment. When we find ourselves hounded by feelings of hopelessness for more than a few weeks, it's important to immediately seek help. There have been great strides in the treatment of depression in recent years — about 80 percent of people are helped. Seeking help for depression is a powerful moral act for a parent. We can, too, encourage spouses, relatives, and friends who are parents to seek help when they exhibit these symptoms. Because the depressed are often both resistant to treatment and emotionally and physically depleted, sometimes they need to be accompanied through the many small steps needed to make and sustain a relationship with a mental health professional.

As parents, we can also talk to our children about our destructive moods. Parents rarely talk to their children not only about depression but about other destructive feelings, often for good reasons. Children certainly don't need to hear about all our downswings or to be regularly tracking our feelings. Whether and how we discuss our moods should depend on many factors — including a child's age, how we imagine our child will interpret this information, and our child's particular vulnerabilities. But when we find ourselves irritable or angry for reasons that do not have to do with our children, or when we are seriously withdrawn, we have a responsibility at least to tell them directly that they are not to blame. As Beardslee's work suggests, often it's less the severity or duration of parents' destructive moods that are damaging to children than how children understand these moods — especially whether they see themselves as the source of the bad mood. As twenty-one-year-old Matt, a deep-feeling soul who grew up with a mother beset by waxing and waning depression, told me: "I used to think my mother just hated being my mother, that she wanted to be doing something else. Now I'm looking back over all those years and seeing them differently and I'm feeling a lot better. I'm seeing that all that anger was coming from something inside of her head. She was depressed. It was about *her*. It didn't have anything to do with me."

Children also need to know that parents are trying to handle their destructive moods responsibly. A parent might say to a teenager: "I've been in a bad mood because I've been fighting with someone I work with. It's not your problem, but I wanted you to understand why I've been snapping a lot. If I continue to be irritable, I'll get help."

What's more, whenever we find ourselves interacting destructively with our children or struggling to take their perspectives, whenever our children consistently express disrespect for us or whenever we find ourselves disliking them, we should ask ourselves what ghosts might be visiting us, what relationships we might be reproducing. By looking inward and reflecting with trusted family members and friends, we can discover a great deal about the many hidden circumstances that shape our parenting. That reflection may, in turn, require getting some time away from our children as well as finding relief from daily stresses.

Self-awareness, to be sure, is often not enough. Rita knows that her anger toward her son Wayne is fueled by anger toward other men, but she can't stop lashing out at him. Sometimes in these circumstances deliberate plans and contracts with ourselves, among other strategies, can help. Whenever Rita becomes angry at Wayne—when she overhears Wayne trashing a girl on the phone, for instance—she might contract with herself to not talk to him about it for at least one day and to consult with a trusted friend in the meantime. We will also need the courage and the discipline to get feedback from our loved ones about whether our behavior has actually improved. Sometimes family therapy is needed—especially when parents like Rita are so angry and enmeshed with their children. Such therapy commonly teaches family members how to avoid destructive relationship patterns by stepping outside of a relationship—becoming a "bystander"—and helps parents understand how their relationships in their families of origin shape their own families.

It will clearly be hard for many of us to suddenly take this kind of introspective stance, especially because our culture provides so little support for adult moral growth and so few ways for parents to gain wisdom about their own moral development. While some adults belong to religious institutions that regularly engage them in serious moral reflection and cultivate moral awareness, such experiences remain uncommon. Books and talk-show experts fail to alert parents to the dangers of moral regression or to opportunities for moral growth. In the literature and research on parenting and families, children are always evolving but parents rarely change. Nor do experts tend to conceive of parenting as a messy, interactive relationship with a child or help parents understand the many sources of turbulence that can make them deaf to a child's experience.

Yet to fail to engage in this introspection itself sends a smug message to our children, that morality is something that passively and mysteriously arrives with age—"like gray hair and attenuated muscles," as educators David Weber and Harvard Knowles put it—that morality is not something hard-won. Children ought to observe what our great dramatists have sought to teach since ancient times: that moral clarity is often painfully dug out of the mud of many conflicting interests and truths, that moral action is often a matter of doggedly wrestling with our own flaws and demons. Further, this introspection is vital not only to children's morality but often to both parents' and children's well-being. The tragedy of Rita and Wayne is that Rita's failure to appreciate Wayne, and her strategies for protecting herself, badly damage a relationship that is vital not only to Wayne's moral growth but to both Rita's and Wayne's happiness.

It would, of course, be far cleaner just to provide our children with a hard diet of moral messages. But that diet will never get us where we need to go—toward understanding how our own unfolding story as adults is interwoven with the story of our own developing children. For it is often in that dual narrative that children's moral qualities are shaped.

6

THE REAL MORAL POWER OF SCHOOLS

IT IS THE SPRING of my son's sophomore year in high school, and my wife and I find ourselves hustling from classroom to classroom for our parent-teacher conferences, trying to protect our allotted fifteen minutes with each of his five teachers. With three children, we are veterans of this dance, but this evening I find myself battling desolation. It's not that my son is struggling in school or suffering a serious problem; it's that the two teachers we have met thus far have taken us through roughly the same dreary ritual. The teacher begins the session by pulling out a sheet of paper. She recites my son's test scores or grades, and then makes a comment about his being distracted at times and not listening. That "not listening" hangs in the air. I find myself bristling. Is it a euphemism of some kind? Does she find my child difficult? She then reassures us that he is a "good kid."

I don't sense that either of these teachers truly knows my son or cares about what my wife and I are hoping for and fretting about or what we think will help him learn. I know that he does not like one of these teachers and that in his opinion one of these classes is "hell." Yet neither teacher seems to have a clue about his experience.

Then we meet with a third teacher. She starts off the session by telling us how much she enjoys having our son in her class. She describes his willingness to risk being "dumb" by asking questions for the whole class, taking one for the team. She tells us when and how he is confident and when and how he is tentative. She describes his easy relationships with a wide range of classmates and his desire to be helpful. She also talks about his being distracted at times. Yet one of her explanations for this behavior—that any kind of repetitive task is hard for him—helps me understand something about my son that has been opaque to me. She tells us that he never interrupts her or is rude. She asks us how we think he is doing and if we have any concerns, and she listens carefully to our thoughts. I feel that we are in a common project together, a project that is academic but also moral—the project of raising a whole person and a good person. I have to resist the temptation to envelop her in a bear hug.

The American public schools were conceived not solely as an engine of academic success. They were intended chiefly to cultivate in children a certain ideal of character. Public schools were charged with responsibility for taking rising waves of poor urban and immigrant children and molding them into responsible, upright citizens.

Today the expectation that schools will cultivate character is again widespread and deep. The American public, deeply concerned about the failure of children to absorb key values from their parents, sees schools as the next best hope. Polls show that about 70 percent of public school parents want schools to teach "strict standards of right and wrong," and 85 percent want schools to teach values. Research suggests that many stretched-thin parents have also come to doubt their capacities as mentors and are looking to schools to take greater responsibility for their children's character development.

Schools have responded to this demand in a variety of ways. Legions of American schools have invested in packaged "character education" programs of one kind or another—a billion-dollar industry has cropped up in the last several years to inculcate values in the young through schools and other organizations—programs that tout values such as discipline, self-control, responsibility for others, and fairness. What schools call character education is also often a hodgepodge of interventions crafted in response to high-profile problems. A frightening episode of violence in a community spurs, for instance, a violence-prevention program. As a result, within a single school district can be found one school whose idea of moral education is developing civic knowledge and skills, another forming good habits, another drilling on a "virtue of the week," another emphasizing drug-abuse prevention, another building self-esteem, another violence prevention, and another promoting appropriate sexual behavior.

There is often value in these programs. They can clearly help students to reinforce values and moral habits, and sometimes these programs curb troubling behaviors. But there is another stark truth: schools have been trying variations of these programs for decades without fundamentally changing students' moral prospects.

That's because these programs typically have no impact on what matters most. At the crux of children's moral development is not, as I described in the introduction to the book, simply teaching values. It's the moral and mentoring capacities of both teachers and parents. In a school setting, it's also the degree to which teachers and parents can strengthen each other in their very different moral-mentoring roles. Yet parent-teacher relationships tend to be neglected by character-education efforts. And while many teachers are strong moral mentors, others lack the commitment and skills to mentor students effectively or to positively shape students' relationships with one another.

In an era when schools are under the gun to improve student performance, administrators are understandably looking for quick fixes and shortcuts. Yet there are no straightforward or easy ways for schools to develop powerful moral capacities in children, and children tend to sniff out exactly how half-baked most character-education programs are. If we are serious about promoting children's moral development in schools, it's critical to focus on *adult* development—on the mentoring and moral capacities of teachers and parents—and on how parents and teachers can work together far more constructively. Why do these relationships so commonly go awry? What can be done to make schools places where we as adults—both teachers and parents—are not simply, as educators David Weber and Harvard Knowles put it, more adept than students "at manipulating the rhetoric of morality," but instead examine our values, moral abilities, and attitudes; reflect on the school as a moral environment; look closely at our relationships with children; and critically examine what we are doing—and not doing—to assure that children grow up to be good people in the world? What can be done to make these relationships between teachers and children and parents and teachers powerful vehicles for both adults' and children's moral growth?

THE PARENT-TEACHER RELATIONSHIP

David Stone, a tall, slightly mischievous man, has been a beloved teacher in a junior high school in a middle-class Boston suburb for over twenty years. But he has recently decided to leave the profession. When I meet with him, he is agitated and still jobless, but he has no regrets. His decision, he tells me, was prompted by one factor alone. "I couldn't deal with parents anymore. Parents are out of control." One parent who was upset about her son's grades insisted that she read every paper in the class to see if he had been graded fairly. Another parent, whose son was outright rude, encouraged him simply to ignore David when he tried to discipline him. A third parent asked him to overlook his daughter's plagiarism. The worst for him, though, were parents who "were always seeking an advantage for their child"—parents who wanted him to give their child extra attention, or who pushed the school to provide more "gifted" classes for their intelligent child. "It's a dog fight. A lot of parents are just advocating for their kid and they don't care about how they might be hurting other kids."

There are great advantages when teachers and parents can work in concert: there are large risks when they cannot. Parents and teachers can clearly be more effective if they agree on what values are important to promote and on how to promote them, yet the best parent-teacher relationships are not just about promoting generic values. In the strongest relationships, parents and teachers mentor each other and achieve something wonderful—a kind of pure focus, uncluttered by their own issues and agendas, on the needs and interests of a child, as the third teacher at our son's parent-teacher conferences did with my wife and me. In these relationships, parents and teachers can also pool their knowledge to understand the many interacting factors that may undermine a child's capacity for caring or responsibility. Ten-year-old Grace, for example, is furious with her mother after her parents' divorce. At school, she has become increasingly disruptive and rude: she writes on the chalkboard that her teacher is a bitch. To her teacher, who doesn't know about the divorce, these attacks have come from out of the blue. At war with both her parents and her teacher, Grace looks to her peers for support. Other students, however, find her needy and demanding, and their withdrawal only makes her more disruptive. Whether Grace comes out of this experience more or less selfish and more or less able to control destructive feelings will depend a great deal on her teacher's and parents' ability to piece together their different perspectives on her home, school, and peer environments and on how her particular vulnerabilities are triggered by these environments. Sometimes teachers also need to integrate a parent's entirely different cultural perspective, and vice versa.

Yet these kinds of parent-teacher relationships are not typical. Often teachers never form any real alliance with parents because they fear that getting below the surface will stir up conflict. The great educator John Dewey was a fierce enemy of the politeness and formalism that typifies the parent-teacher relationship. Some teachers, especially high school teachers, don't see it as their job to work closely with parents in order to understand a child. Many teachers are so stressed and overextended that they fall back on reciting test scores, as the first two teachers did at my son's parent-teacher conferences. Other teachers are highly guarded because they are keenly aware of the tremendous responsibility they bear and worry a great deal about disappointing parents: "Parent-teacher conferences are by far the most stressful times of the year for me," a warm, intelligent teacher, who is also a parent, said to me. "I feel that it is an awesome responsibility and honor to teach a child. Parents are handing over responsibility for their child's learning to me. And it's terrifying to think that I might fail or even be perceived as failing." Some parents, especially low-income parents, are also suspicious of schools—they often have bad memories of their own time as students—or don't feel entitled to advocate for their children in schools.

Yet in middle- and upper-class communities, the kinds of overbearing, micromanaging parents that David describes are an even bigger problem—these parents not only fail to collaborate with teachers but sometimes model for children fundamental disrespect. Soon after talking to David I spoke with another revered educator—a teacher for twenty years and then a principal for five years in an affluent community in Connecticut—who had left the profession for similar reasons. "Parents would call me with commands. I remember this dad who ordered me to place his child in a classroom with a teacher he thought was the best. I told him I couldn't do that. He told me: 'You have to or I'll be in your office tomorrow with the superintendent.'" Other teachers complain about parents who seem to want to have their fingers in every aspect of the classroom experience. One suburban teacher told me that she will never forgive a parent who got on her knees and sniffed her classroom rug to see if it was producing odors that might be bothersome to her child. Psychologist and school consultant Michael Thompson says that sometimes what teachers want is for children to have a "parentectomy."

And it's not just blatantly obnoxious, micromanaging parents. Many parents—many of us—in subtle, unintended ways can create unreasonable burdens on teachers. I know that I have experienced a kind of tunnel vision when it comes to my children and have lost sight of teachers' perspectives. I recently heard a teacher complain about parents who try to talk to her when they drop off their child in the morning, a critical period for her in preparing for class. I felt the sting of recognition—I had done this more than once. Teachers complain about parents who try to befriend them as a way of currying favor for their child and about parents who hang around the classroom a great deal, scrutinizing them and peppering them with suggestions. In affluent communities, especially, teachers can feel that they are under parents' microscope, that every aspect of their practice, as Thompson observes, is being dissected by what is now called "the Volvo caucus." What adds insult to injury is that teachers can feel judged by adults whom they see, as the author and educator Sara Lawrence-Lightfoot puts it, as biased and without the competence to judge them.

And while I have known many, many parents who have deep concerns about students other than their own—parents who go to great lengths, for example, to help teachers find tutors or other resources for other students who are struggling—I have also known significant numbers of parents who are narrowly focused on their own children and take little responsibility for other children in the classroom or the larger school community. "We have a lot of parents who care about other kids," says Elaine, a mother who heads a parent council in a well-known independent school in Washington, D.C. "But we also have a good number of parents who don't seem to have any consciousness whatsoever that their child is not the only child in the building." Some parents have little tolerance in particular for other children who may be compromising their own child's learning. I have talked to parents who are outraged when a child with a behavior problem is disrupting their child's learning. "I couldn't believe they didn't just kick the kid out," a parent whose child attends a highly respected independent school in Manhattan recently said to me. "I'm paying a fortune for my kid to go to this school, and another kid is interfering with her learning? It doesn't make any sense." (How a parent should respond in this situation, as I take up later, is a complex issue.)

Moreover, even when the number of these parents is small, they can determine the tone and quality of school staffs' interactions with all parents. Many independent and suburban schools, partly in response to a relatively small number of demanding parents, develop policies and practices that keep parents at arm's length. These schools have numerous parent open houses, for example, but the events are carefully scripted.

Finally, the troubling reality is that even when parents are community-minded and trying very hard to work collaboratively with teachers, the parent-teacher relationship can go awry, for many reasons. Parents can clearly be raw and defensive when they receive from teachers explicit or tacit criticism of their parenting, as I was when two teachers said my son had trouble listening. These meetings with teachers may be the only place, in fact, where parents ever hear criticism of their parenting. Often at bottom what parents want is for teachers to simply know and like their child, and when teachers talk only about performance or fail to express affection or praise, parents can feel cheated and shaken.

This relationship can also stir up in us as parents competitive feelings, and issues with authority and attachment. We may bridle because our relationship with a teacher feels too intimate—we may hear that our child has exposed, for example, private details of our home life. Some parents may feel threatened by children's close relationships with their teachers. A cold teacher or a slight or manipulation in our contact with a teacher, real or imagined, can also send us reeling back, in ways we are often not conscious of, to times when as children we felt mistreated by authority figures, including our parents, or to times we felt unappreciated or mistreated as students—to the "ghosts in the classroom," as Sara Lawrence-Lightfoot puts it.

Some teachers, on the other hand, chose their profession because they have difficulties working closely with adults, especially adults in positions of power. Some teachers also overidentify with children, hindering their capacity to take parents' perspective.

CREATING STRONG PARENT-TEACHER ALLIANCES

These parent-teacher issues have many layers and can be dealt with in various ways—strategies that will differ not only depending on whether a school is rich or poor but on many other parent, school, and community characteristics. But there are common stances and strategies that can make a large difference across all schools.

Schools can do much more to engage a wide range of parents, including difficult parents. Hard as it is for any teacher or administrator to deal with pushy, obnoxious parents, no school that is serious about moral development can simply keep them at bay, precisely because it is these parents whose children are likely to be at greatest moral risk. Schools do not have to set out to fundamentally change these parents. But they can provide teachers with ongoing support and guidance in working with them, including helping teachers avoid easy finger-pointing and scapegoating and manage class biases. It's important for teachers to see in particular that beneath parents who come across as arrogant and entitled are often fearful, isolated human beings who may be terrified of handing over their child to a stranger or of losing control of their child.

In every type of school it is also possible to engage parents in a moral community that pushes parents to look beyond their own children. That means, in part, finding multiple ways for parents to be engaged in a school—as classroom volunteers, on parent councils, as members of teams devoted to particular projects. And it means that schools need to articulate clearly their moral goals and expectations for both parents and students through moral charters—clear, visible statements of a school's values. More important, these charters cannot just collect dust or become part of the scenery, their typical fate. They need to live and breathe not only in classrooms but in every aspect of school life.

My children attended a public elementary school that brought both parents and children into a kind of moral community. Interactions with teachers, school events, posters on walls, and communications from our principal worked to connect parents both to one another and to the school. The communications expressed a set of moral commitments—that both parents and children are members of a community and have responsibility for all members of that community; that every student has intellectual and personal contributions to make to the learning of the whole community and that the school has responsibilities to recognize and support those contributions; that school is preparation not only for a career but for many facets of citizenship; that diversity is a high value and that diverse opinions will be engaged and tested; that students should be taught to identify and address social inequities and injustice. Our parent-teacher conferences often did not focus solely on our own child but on how our child might be helpful to other children in the classroom, as well as on schoolwide concerns and the possible roles parents could play in helping deal with those concerns. Often homework was connected to issues of equity and fairness, and sometimes children were asked to engage parents in this homework. Teachers felt responsibility for all children in the building—not just children in their classroom—and went out of their way to work with children who were marginalized and struggling and to engage the parents of those children. Recently this school was asked to merge with another school with large numbers of children who are academically struggling, a challenge that most schools would be skittish about: this school staff openly embraced this challenge and encouraged parents to embrace it. Because there are trusting, caring relationships between teachers and students at this school, children are also more likely to value what teachers value, including classic virtues such as honesty and courage. At the same time, as the principal observes, "Many parents challenge the larger community to believe in and value each of our students and families. This initiative by families reinforces and sometimes helps lead the school to live up to its values."

For our part as parents, there are many ways that we can work to create a moral community and improve our relationships with teachers. We can think, for one, about how we can work more effectively with teachers we don't admire. The point is not that we should learn to admire all teachers or feign admiration for our children's sake—sometimes it's crucial, in fact, for a parent to confirm a child's reality when a teacher is ineffective or inappropriate in some way. But we can be mindful of stresses and challenges that face teachers every day and we can help children understand these stresses. It may help us in empathizing with teachers and in cultivating this empathy in our children to remember, for example, that teachers often feel unsupported by administrators—some teachers in independent schools in particular fear that administrators can't back them up if tuition-paying parents want their heads—that teachers often feel devalued in our culture, and that teachers must regularly contend with attacks from parents on their fundamental ability to do work to which they have brought their souls.

As parents, we can also think through how to advocate for our child while considering the needs of other children. While in many circumstances advocating for the welfare of our children and other children are intimately tied—"Children tend to flourish in communities," as one high school administrator put it, "with other children who are flourishing"—there are circumstances when the needs of our own and other children *do* collide. The parent who is concerned about another child in the class who has a behavior problem is not simply hardhearted; children who are aggressive or who have difficulty controlling their impulses can badly undermine the learning of other children. Often parents are in real ethical dilemmas, having to sort through the complexities of actions that may benefit their child but hurt others, or vice versa.

Yet here again there is an opportunity to demonstrate an important form of morality. The point is not that we as parents should put other children's needs before those of our own children. The point is that we act morally and model that morality for our children in a school setting when we struggle with the tension between what is best for our child and what is best for other children. Ultimately, it may make sense, for example, for a parent to advocate for a gifted class or to urge that a child who is constantly disruptive or draining for others be removed from a classroom. But rather than moving quickly to seek expulsion for this child, we as parents can model for our children compassion for the child, encourage a teacher to find constructive ways to work with the child, urge school administrators to provide teachers with adequate forms of support in this work, and signal in conversations with other parents some sense of collective responsibility for all children in the community. Before we lobby for a gifted class, we should at least find out what a school might have to sacrifice to provide the class or how else those resources might be used.

For both teachers and parents, it's critical to take a third-person perspective when the parent-teacher relationship becomes defensive or antagonistic. For us as parents, a trusted, engaged listener — a friend, spouse, or relative — can help us sort through how we can ally with a teacher and what our goals are in this relationship, so we don't come to it either shut down or loaded for bear.

Finally, there are very specific, concrete things that both schools and parents across various settings can do to avert finger-pointing and to create the conditions that make strong relationships possible. In parent-teacher conferences it can help, for instance, when parents start a session by reporting something positive that a child has said about a teacher. When teachers, for their part, start a parent-teacher conference by identifying a distinct strength of a child—and explain how that strength expresses itself in a classroom, as my son's teacher did with my wife and me—they can set a parent-teacher conference on a wholly different path than if they recite test scores or immediately zero in on problems. As a teacher points out to Sara Lawrence-Lightfoot, it also helps if teachers can use "we" with parents—not "What are you going to do?" or "What am I going to do?" in moving a child forward or responding to a child's difficulty, but "What are *we* going to do?"—in order to establish a constructive alliance.

TEACHER-STUDENT RELATIONSHIPS

A high school student recently sent me an excerpt from her blog:

> *When teachers and students came together two weeks ago to talk about ways to encourage participation, moral decisions were like silent shadows in the room. When one teacher made a joke— "You mean humiliation is a bad thing?"— we all laughed because we were all there to learn from each other, to make the classroom a better place, but at the same time, it reminded me of plenty of instances of witnessing, or hearing about, humiliation of students. And plenty of times where the teacher could've used humiliation, but chose to take another route. [This] might seem pretty bent out of shape coming from a student, but students notice when teachers make moral decisions; whether it be to admit to a mistake, encourage all students to participate, or have classroom decisions be made transparent. It can brighten my day or ruin it.*

Janet Rimer, a third-year teacher in rural Illinois, spent a good deal of the spring semester worrying about one of her students, twelve-year-old Mathias. Bright, tense, quick to ignite with both her and other students, early in the semester Mathias seemed to have mentally bailed out of school completely, and he got into petty fights with his classmates almost constantly. Janet refused to give up on him. She pressed him to complete his homework and held him to a high standard, yet quickly encouraged him when he took even the smallest steps forward. By the end of the semester he had made some academic progress. But he never expressed any kind of thanks, and Janet still despaired about whether she had reached him. Would he be back to square one next year?

At the end of the semester, while cleaning out her students' desks, she removed some scraps of paper from inside Mathias's desk. On one scrap a sentence was scrawled that pierced her to the core: "Whoever gets to sit in this desk, you should know that this teacher really cares."

During the past two decades, I have spent time in dozens of schools and talked to scores of students. I have observed again and again students' exquisite sensitivity to the qualities of their teachers — both their fierce loyalty to teachers they trust and their razor-sharp alertness to hypocrisy, injustice, indifference. Research shows that even when schools undergo major restructuring, students tend to pay little attention to these changes — they still focus on the strengths and weaknesses of individual teachers. It is still teachers who earn their admiration, trust, distrust, disdain.

These relationships can influence children's moral qualities in many ways. Teachers do not, in fact, get to choose whether they influence students' character. Teachers are inevitably and always influencing children's moral attitudes and capacities, for better or worse, by what they choose to praise and punish, how fairly they balance different students' needs, what they value, how they define students' obligations to each other. Teachers are always affecting the emotions underpinning students' moral development. Teachers can make children radioactive with shame, as the student writing in her blog indicates, or they can model empathy. And just as parents and children are in a reciprocal relationship—with parents affecting children's emotional and moral lives and children affecting parents' emotional and moral lives—teachers and children can influence each other in complex reverberations that are often positive but sometimes clearly destructive. Randall, a seventh grader I interviewed in Little Rock, Arkansas, who gets under everyone's skin, finds himself in a common kind of escalating war with adults. His constant antagonism makes it hard for school staff to see his perspective and even brings out in them a primitive anger—one teacher calls him "a jerk," and the principal refers to him as "that little asshole"—which only seems to make him step up his provocations, further enraging his teachers and the principal. Randall is spinning out of his school community. When I ask him whom he trusts, he holds up a piece of paper that is totally blank.

But how can teachers purposefully develop children's moral qualities? Teachers can instill moral habits, scaffold hope and idealism, directly promote appreciation and respect for others, challenge students to be better. Teachers can draw out in children their many moral questions: Should I back up my best friend during a fight, even though I know he is wrong? Should I tell the school counselor that my mother or father is seriously depressed or drinking too much or angry all the time, or is that betraying my family? Should I tell an adult if a popular student steals a calculator from another student, knowing that I could end up a social leper? Like parents, teachers are most effective in these conversations when they stand for important values, while listening responsively and entering children's worlds. Simple listening can be, for some children who are accustomed to dealing with stressed-out teachers, like water in a desert. In the poem "The Parent Conference," the teacher and poet Mary Burchenal describes a fruitless, glum parent-teacher-counselor-student session that suddenly takes a different turn when she simply asks the student: "When does baseball season start?"

While large numbers of teachers clearly have the motivation and skills to be this kind of moral educator, many teachers lack them. Many teachers, especially high school teachers, are also simply failing to earn students' basic trust and respect, making effective mentoring impossible.

These failures have several roots. Many teachers—again especially high school teachers—don't see their jobs as involving moral education or forming relationships with students. Even when teachers do embrace the moral-educator role, they often simply "teach values." There is often, too, a high wall that separates the culture of students and the culture of adults in a school building. No other adult is better positioned to understand the world of children than teachers, yet often teachers have little idea about how students experience school, what students value, who's bullying or excluding whom. Further, it might increase students' empathy for and improve their relationships with teachers to know basic facts about their teachers—why teachers have chosen their profession, how they are trained, the stresses they face.

Many urban teachers especially are frayed by disillusionment and stress, which corrode exactly those qualities—empathy, persistence, consistency, moral energy—that are crucial to shepherding students' moral growth. "As a human, I may never be up to this," a Boston teacher recently said to me. Disillusionment and stress are prime reasons that teachers are leaving the profession in droves—somewhere between 40 and 50 percent of new teachers across the country will leave the profession within their first five years. "New teachers come to our school who've seen too many movies about a teacher, played by Michelle Pfeifer or Robin Williams, who comes in and rescues kids," a seasoned, widely admired urban high school teacher told me. "And pretty soon they realize that kids don't change that easily, and these teachers get wiped out."

Yet there may be a bigger obstacle to teachers' developing these relationship capacities and mentoring skills across many different types of communities. Like other adults, many teachers have a fundamental misconception about their moral and mentoring capacities. They often see these capacities as set in stone. Many teachers don't see themselves as working to become more fair or more generous or better able to appreciate students' perspectives. Often when students transgress, the reflex of teachers and other administrators is to simply tighten or create more rules and step up punishments—it's not to reflect on whether the school community functions in a way that makes a transgression more likely or on their own flaws, biases, and errors. Nor are these transgressions typically used as "teachable moments," as opportunities to engage students in understanding why the transgression occurred, how it impacted others, and why certain moral standards exist. (Recall the example of Lisa in chapter 1.)

There are, in fact, many opportunities for teachers to deepen their appreciation, to overcome biases, and to acquire important moral understanding in their relationships with their students. This potential hit me several years ago, in talking to a friend who was then a high school teacher. He had embarked with his students on a discussion of religion, and in the course of the discussion he remarked casually that he didn't believe in God. One of his students approached him after class, visibly vexed. She told him that she was a religious person and that his comment was incomprehensible to her. "How can I respect your judgment and guidance," she asked, "if it's not rooted in a belief in God?"

The incident forced this teacher to ask crucial questions about his effectiveness as a moral mentor. It brought home to him a certain kind of egocentrism—how much did he really understand about his students' perspectives? It spurred him to reflect specifically on the vast differences in the foundation of his own and some of his students' moral beliefs. And it engaged him in thinking about a hard question at the center of teaching values that many teachers never think about—how to connect that teaching to the specific moral orientations of his students.

I have talked to teachers in wealthy schools who have worked to overcome their prejudices about privileged children, including their knee-jerk assumption that these children are spoiled. One teacher told me that she was enraged at one of her students and his parents because he was skipping class with his parents' permission to hit the links. "But after I got angry, I thought, how sad is this, parents letting their kid skip school to play golf."

CREATING A MORAL SCHOOL COMMUNITY

Yet the burden should not fall on simply isolated teachers to work on their moral and mentoring capacities. To promote children's moral growth, schools need to become very different kinds of places. As parents concerned about our children's moral development, we should be asking ourselves whether a school supports and cultivates the moral and mentoring capacities of adults as well as children, pays careful attention to teachers' relationships with parents and students' relationships with teachers, and seeks to break down the wall that separates the cultures of students and adults in schools.

Schools can take concrete steps to identify students who are un-anchored to any adult—and who are most at risk of moral troubles—and to create ties for them to school staff. As education journalist Nancy Walser reports, at an annual staff meeting at the Bowman Elementary School in Anchorage, Alaska, paper stars, each with a student's name, are posted on the wall, and staff members put their names next to the stars of every student with whom they have a significant relationship. The school then makes sure that staff members check in with isolated students on a regular basis, even if it's just a casual conversation. Partly because of this intervention, more students, data suggest, are attached to an adult. An independent high school outside of Boston went through a similar process and found that almost every teacher had a connection to the same group of girls, but that many boys had no connection to a teacher.

In schools that are serious about moral development, administrators will also work hard to hire teachers who are interested in students' moral growth, to reduce stresses on teachers, and to give teachers opportunities to reflect on their successes and failures as moral mentors. Teachers need chances to reflect, for example, on why they can't summon a particle of empathy or even feel contempt for some students like Randall, on why certain students don't trust and respect them, and on their own moral questions and errors, and how to talk to students about those errors.

At the same time, as parents we should urge schools to encourage children to express their concerns to teachers when they feel mistreated and to provide teachers with guidance in responding to these concerns constructively. It also often makes sense to include children in parent-teacher conferences—a new practice in some schools. Guidance counselors can also meet with students and teachers together and encourage students to voice concerns.

What makes so much of what passes as character education these days irrelevant—when it is not altogether a travesty—is that it has no impact on adults' capacity to meet these crucial challenges. Worse, these programs not only don't influence teachers' mentoring or moral qualities; they can reinforce the idea that teachers and other adults are already highly morally evolved and simply have to transplant their values into their students.

Improving teacher-student and parent-teacher relationships is not a panacea, and there is much else that schools ought to do. For example, students should read about and interact with moral exemplars, men and women of strong conviction who are working to improve the world, and they should have opportunities in many aspects of the curriculum to reflect on values and to mull over moral dilemmas and questions, especially those that emerge from their daily experience. At Cambridge Rindge and Latin High

School in Massachusetts, a group of students every year creates dramatic presentations that explore community-wide social and ethical concerns, such as, Should I snitch on a good friend who is stealing from the store where he works? A few character-education programs, such as the Child Development Project, based in Oakland, California, and Open Circle, based outside of Boston, also guide teachers in creating a democratic community—children do structured exercises that help them take the perspectives of other children and they have opportunities to create rules for the community, to solve classroom problems, to determine sanctions. Children are far more likely to embrace a rule or value when instead of having that rule or value dictated to them by an adult, they come to it through their more prized capacity—their ability to think. Schools also can be alert to and seek to counter the "hidden" moral curriculum. Many kinds of school practices—academic tracking, special-needs placements, disciplinary actions, curriculum choices—send moral messages to students that can be constructive or destructive, messages especially about adults' conceptions of and commitments to justice as well as messages about how adults view children. As character-education expert Thomas Lickona puts it: "You don't have an adequate character-education program if you've still got a mind-deadening curriculum that doesn't respect children as learners or a program that tracks students into winners and losers." Well-structured, meaningful community-service opportunities, and opportunities for older students to mentor younger students, can also bolster key moral qualities.

Much of this work will be difficult, especially in the large number of schools where preparing students for high-stakes tests is gobbling up teachers' energy and time. But we can't keep falling back on the usual character-education bromides. What's more, most of the things that are crucial to supporting children's moral development in schools—creating strong communities, assuring that children have a trusting relationship with an adult, developing solid connections between teachers and parents, fighting teacher stagnation and promoting teachers' growth—are also absolutely crucial to children's academic development. And unlike so many other character-education efforts, this work stands a real chance of developing in children the qualities they need to be kind and responsible adults.

7

THE MORALLY MATURE SPORTS PARENT

IN CONDUCTING RESEARCH FOR THIS BOOK—and I spoke to parents from many parts of this country as well as from Canada and Australia—there was nothing easier than to find stories about parents who acted like idiots at children's sporting events. I heard about a father who brings a stopwatch to games so that he can monitor exactly how many minutes his son plays relative to other players and who badgers the coach with this data if his son has been slighted; about two mothers of opposing teams smacking each other with their purses in the stands; about parents at hockey games who spit on opposing players in the rink. A report by the National Alliance for Youth Sports includes these heartwarming stories: two women assaulting and leaving unconscious a mother after a youth baseball game in Utah; a youth baseball coach in Wisconsin being arrested for wrestling an umpire to the ground; and over thirty adults brawling at the end of a soccer tournament for players under the age of fourteen in Los Angeles.

More than 40 million American children are engaged in organized sports—outside of home and school, adults interact with children the most at these events. And children's sports are now widely hyped as helping children avoid drugs, crime, and gang involvement and as helping children develop many virtues such as courage, fairness, and responsibility. Talk about children's sports is now utterly saturated with moral talk.

There's no question that children's sports can have all sorts of morally helpful influences, and not just in developing virtues or in keeping children out of harm's way. Sports can help children manage shame and anger and develop moral reasoning. Decisions in sports about, say, whether to stand out individually or promote teammates and about what constitutes fair play have numerous parallels in other areas of life. Sports can help children learn how to contribute their particular talents to a community, and furnish children, as political scientist Michael Gillespie puts it, with a "concrete experience of justice." Unlike other social spheres, sports are a true meritocracy. Children compete on a level playing field—who wins or loses is not a matter of connections or status but of skill, intelligence, and perseverance. Pickup sports, as Gillespie observes, because they require coordination of interests in a momentary community, can also help children develop democratic "political" skills.

Nor is it a small matter that sports are the only time these days when some children have contact with their fathers or when they receive the careful, undivided attention of male mentors. Because schools are so often segregated—and because children are so commonly in different classes and on separate tracks within schools—sports are also sometimes the only arena where children have the opportunity to develop friendships and understanding of others across race, ethnicity, and class. On countless football and baseball fields and basketball courts across this country, white children are coming to understand for the first time something about how children of color think and feel, and vice versa.

Yet this much is equally incontrovertible: these opportunities are routinely squandered, and children's sports can be a feel-good, moral charade, an occasion for all kinds of inflated moral rhetoric that masks outright destruction to children's developing morality. Sports can feed a mob mentality, fuel children's self-righteousness, amplify their sense that all that matters is their own feelings, reinforce their tendency to invent enemies. Too many times as a coach, a parent, and a child playing sports myself, the only lesson I have seen children draw from sporting events is that the referee is an idiot and members of the other team are some lower form of life. As much as we extol the virtues of sports, it is not, it is vital to underline, sports per se that builds children's character.

While the effects of sports on children's moral development depend on many factors, there are two that are most central. First, adults in different communities use sports to advance very different values and developmental goals. While parents and coaches in some communities prize courage and toughness, for example, parents in other communities put a premium on social skills and self-esteem. And these different values create different moral benefits and risks for children.

Second, the moral benefits and costs of sports depend on how parents and coaches relate to each other and on how coaches and parents relate to children. That significant numbers of parents and coaches are acting recklessly is, of course, no trivial concern. But it's wrong to define the problem only in terms of this relatively small fraction of adults. As is the case with academic achievement, the problem is not simply "them"—a group of immature, uncorked parents. Nor is it simply fanatic coaches. Despite our positive intentions, many of us as parents and coaches, if we are honest with ourselves, are not at our best at children's sports events. Many of us bring to these events unresolved, often subtle conflicts and hopes that can cause us to lose perspective on a child's interests and fail to model for children basic respect and responsibility for others.

How do ideologies and values concerning sports differ across communities, and what are the consequences for children? Why do so many of us regress at these events and how can we as parents and coaches both mentor more effectively and work more constructively with each other? Finally, what can be done to bring the wisdom of innovative sports programs—programs that create important opportunities for adults' and children's moral learning to communities across the country?

THE MEANING OF SPORTS IN AMERICAN COMMUNITIES

Jeff and I are leaning against a fence, enjoying one of the wonders of late spring — watching our children play baseball on a glorious early evening, the sun gently lifting off the grass. Jeff, a former computer salesman who has been unemployed for a few months, is a parent of an eight-year-old, Sam. Sam is playing Little League for the first time. I don't know Jeff well, but he seems affable and outgoing.

What is clear is that, for Jeff, Sam's introduction to Little League is momentous. Jeff has emphasized with me how important it is to him that Sam "has fun," but Jeff is intense. He and Sam are the first to get to the field, and because Jeff is looking for some opportunity to talk to the coach, they are often the last to leave. During the games, Jeff paces behind the batter's box. When Sam is batting, Jeff will sometimes pepper him with instructions: "Keep your elbow up!" "Eye on the ball." At times Sam seems visibly annoyed. One time, Jeff interrupts the game to yell at Sam to tie his shoes.

During most games Sam looks pretty miserable, and he tends to be curt with other kids. When he is batting he seems tied in a million knots. His swing is tentative, uneasy, or he lashes at the ball. He is coordinated but not a fluid, natural athlete, and the tension makes it impossible for him to hit effectively. When he bats I have a sinking sense that it will not end well.

This day the umpire again puts the nail in the coffin — *Strike three!* — and Sam heads back to the bench. Jeff comes up behind him — "Shake it off, bud. No big deal. You'll get a hit next time."

Coach Dodson has coached Little League for over twenty-five years. He is a smart, no-nonsense man who takes his work seriously, who expects a great deal from his players, and who doles out compliments grudgingly, as if he is lifting a truck off himself. Today, he gathers his team together after a tough loss in a playoff game. The pitcher, Isaac, has pitched the whole game, gutting out several grueling innings, and he is visibly drained, exhausted.

Coach Dodson applauds the effort of the whole team. But then his attention fixes on Isaac. Isaac, he says, has risen to the occasion, has dug deep within himself. Not once was he intimidated, not once did he let himself get discouraged, even when defeat was near. "That's how you play this game," he pointedly declares to the other players. He walks over to Isaac and hands him the game ball. He leans over slowly and cups the sides of Isaac's head with his hands. He gently kisses Isaac on the forehead. Tears well up in Isaac's eyes.

The legendary anthropologist Clifford Geertz described sports as a kind of "deep play" that expresses the innermost values of a society. For the ancient Greeks, for example, sports were chiefly about individual glory and winning and were forums where adults reenacted struggles tied to the struggles of the gods. For the British, sports historically have been primarily about team loyalty, strict adherence to rules, and honor.

In the United States today, sports reflect not one but roughly two sets of core values. In many communities, including the community where Coach Dodson lives, sports are about perseverance, excellence, courage, toughness, and sacrifice. A high premium is placed not on shielding children from adversity but on helping them overcome it. A friend of mine from rural Pennsylvania told me that in his community, masculinity and character were closely linked to the courage and toughness required to hunt. He didn't like to hunt but he was able to save face by playing football, a barely accepted surrogate. Often in these communities sports are not only seen as cultivating courage and tenacity, they are understood as a test of whether children have these qualities. In this sense, sports are, for children, a kind of audition for life. As the author and journalist Heywood Hale Broun put it: "Sports do not build character, they reveal it." Over and over I have heard coaches, like Coach Dodson, as well as parents, comment on whether children have "poise" or "heart" or "toughness" based on their performance in sports. In many of these communities—but certainly not all—winning is also very important, and high school athletes are often heroes, attracting gaudy attention not only from students but from adults. Sometimes athletes as young as eight years old, playing in informal leagues, attract a great deal of adult attention.

In other communities, including the community in which Jeff lives, adults tend to see sports as developing character by building self-esteem, empathy, and social understanding. A high premium is placed not on dealing with adversity or winning but on co-operation. In one Boston suburb, some children don't play tug of war, they play "tug of peace." Parents typically and quite deliberately ask their children "Did you have fun?" instead of "Did you win?" Not infrequently, I hear parents single out and cartoon other parents as competitive monsters, as a way of firmly establishing how little competition means to them. Sometimes programs for young children don't keep score, and often at the end of the season every child gets a trophy.

While I've described these communities as distinct, the lines between them are often not clear. Communities where friendship and fun are touted tend to be affluent, liberal suburban communities, while communities that prize toughness tend to be working-class and poor. But talk about self-esteem now permeates many types of communities, and talk about toughness can be heard across class. Talented young athletes can magnetize adults in many types of communities. Further, in many communities there are new hybrids of these values, and values can also openly conflict. In the mixed-income town where I live, I once watched a game where a couple of parents praised a Little League pitcher for apologizing to a batter he accidentally hit; other parents saw the parents' praise as a violation of a code and as flat-out encouraging wimpiness. After the game, one of these parents said to me, "What are they going to do next, suggest that every time a batter is hit the kids get together and light candles?" (I heard about a similar incident where a parent said: "What do these parents want the kids to do, hold hands and sing 'Kum Ba Yah'?") A proposal by some parents in my community to use a softer ball so that their children would avoid injury met with similar contempt from another group of parents.

Nevertheless, most children are exposed primarily to one of the two ideologies, with different effects on their moral growth. There are clearly important moral benefits for children in communities that prize toughness and courage. As I argued earlier in this book, in an age where many of us as parents are too focused on shielding our children from adversity, children can morally benefit and thrive when an adult, like Coach Dodson, makes high demands, does *not* attend to their momentary feelings or frequently praise, cherishes their effort, and expresses faith in their capacity to overcome hardship. It can help children morally to be asked to sacrifice, to endure some pain, for a communal goal. My own sons thrived in these circumstances, and I think they felt relief to be around adults who were less attentive to their feelings than I tend to be. (They also had coaches who were unfair and obtuse, and they developed the important capacity to manage these adults.) Further, I certainly know adults who believe that the tenacity and courage that was demanded of them by high school sports has boosted their confidence and reduced their fear in other arenas in their adult life.

Yet while it's one thing to believe that sports can develop these qualities, it's another thing—and quite dangerous—to believe that sports are a test of whether children *have* these qualities, that sports "reveal character," as Broun put it. For in vital respects sports are not a metaphor for life, and functioning in sports does not predict, research suggests, functioning in life. Anyone who spends time with children can also see that many children who act courageously in sports are timid in other areas in life, and many children who are timid in a key moment in a game or have difficulty persevering are quite capable of acting courageously or with tenacity in other arenas. Many children, too, are unwilling to sacrifice in sports but are quite capable of other kinds of sacrifice for other purposes. When we as parents or coaches treat sports as a test of these qualities or as an audition for life, we can wrongly label and categorize children as weak—and children can shamefully label themselves. In cases where the value of toughness is paramount and highly visible and where toughness brings recognition from key adults—when a coach ceremoniously plants a kiss on a pitcher's forehead for being tough—children can also feel that if they are not tough, they are not worthy of appreciation or this kind of love, with all sorts of obvious detrimental consequences.

There are also clear perils in exalting student athletes or simply failing to counteract athletes' perception that they are better than their peers—especially because these revered young people commonly model and set moral norms for their peers and for large numbers of younger children. This kind of attention is not only likely to breed arrogance, it sends a message to other students that can seem utterly perverse and that can undercut adults as mentors. As a Tennessee student wrote on our survey: "I am a great person, and there are many other kids like me, but we don't really get recognized the way athletes do. All they have done is been blessed with skills in a game. A GAME."

Children who grow up in communities where parents downplay winning and preach cooperation and empathy tend, on the other hand, to have far more perspective on the importance of sports—they don't see sports as an audition for life. When competition and winning are downplayed, children who are not athletic may also be more likely to have fun, unscathing experiences and to learn social skills through sports.

Yet children in these communities face other kinds of risks—in particular the risk of viewing parents as hypocrites. When we tell our children that sports are primarily about friendship and fun, when we make a big show of not caring about whether our children perform at a high level, and then, like Jeff, pace on the sidelines, yell out instructions, talk anxiously to coaches, or press children to practice, children cannot help but notice the gulf between our espoused beliefs and our actions. Sometimes, as with parents' messages about academic achievement, children are not conscious of these mixed messages about the importance of performance. They can feel anxious and ashamed without knowing why, and feel ashamed of being ashamed.

Parents' allergy to competition can be harmful as well. I certainly understand this allergy—competition simply makes some children and adults anxious, and many of us have memories of feeling humiliated as children when we failed to live up to our own or some other person's expectations during an emotionally charged, competitive sports event.

Yet most of the important moral benefits from sports accrue not from the absence of competition but precisely from its presence. When adults constantly seek to eliminate competition, they diminish important opportunities for children to bump up against both the intensity of others' feelings and the intensity of their own, opportunities to learn how to manage disappointment, shame, and anger. In healthy competitive sports, children turn perfectly well-meaning strangers or even friends into enemies, and then return them, often at lightning speed, into fellow human beings after a game. And it's precisely in the back-and-forth of making another person a faceless foe and then a fellow human being that children learn to decelerate their aggression. At some level, children may even recognize the irrationality of the antagonism itself, that it is, after all, produced by a game. It's hard to imagine a more powerful deterrent to violating another human being than recognizing that our hostile feelings toward another person are a kind of fiction, manufactured by a game, and have nothing to do with him or her at all—that we irrationally invent enemies. At the same time, children can learn to react appropriately to aggression in others—to neither withdraw in the face of others' aggression or to let their own aggression spiral out of control.

Further, competition provides children the opportunity to develop deep forms of appreciation. Competition challenges children to appreciate the skills of opposing players even when they seem like mortal enemies, to find weaker teammates' strengths even when those players are jeopardizing the team's chances of making the playoffs, to take the referee's perspective, at least after the game, even when he or she makes a bad call at a critical moment. That's the kind of demanding morality that helps to develop over time children's capacity to see beyond their own intense feelings, to tolerate others' flaws, to place others' perspectives and needs on a par with their own.

Increasing the benefits of sports and minimizing the dangers means, then, different things in different communities. It's important for adults in communities that tout social skills and self-esteem to encourage competition, hold children to high standards, and ask children to sacrifice at least in some measure for the team. It's important in communities that prize courage and toughness, on the other hand, for adults to treat sports as only one, relatively unimportant, arena in which children test their qualities, for adults to insist that children attend to the feelings of other children, and for adults to find ways for sports to be gratifying for players who are not naturally courageous or tough in this arena.

Just as important, we as parents can stay closely attuned to what type of sports at what level of intensity will benefit our children. There tend to be great differences in levels of competition between community sports programs and school sports, as well as within community sports and school sports. The goal should not be for every child to experience the same level of moderate competition. Some children can clearly benefit from programs that are highly competitive and encourage toughness, while other children can just as clearly benefit from programs that teach social understanding, and these benefits may change at different points in a child's development. If we can carefully listen to children and take in their experience while playing sports, we can far more effectively guide these decisions.

CHECKING OURSELVES AT SPORTING EVENTS

I am sitting in a high school cafeteria, listening with about thirty other parents to a sports consultant describing the dangers to children of overinvolved sports parents. One parent raises his hand and offers a kind of confession: "I remember my son's last day playing youth soccer. The game was over, and I remember standing out on the field and thinking to myself: 'What am I going to do with my life?'" The audience erupts in warm, knowing laughter.

No matter the values of a community, there are large risks when parents or coaches are too emotionally wrapped up in children's sports—when we depend on children's sports to work out our own conflicts or as a primary source of meaning or for a mood boost. That's not to say that we should fret or beat ourselves up when we have charged, intense feelings at our children's games. It's thrilling to see our children perform well on a public stage; it's understandably distressing when our children fail on that stage. Many of us also become deeply involved in our children's sports because we have invested a great deal of our own time and energy in them: we routinely wake up at an ungodly hour to drive our kids to practices, or we regularly cart them across the state to their games.

But sports can also stir up in us a wide range of feelings—frustration, outrage, anxiety, disappointment, shame—that must be carefully managed. And some parents cross an important line—a line that the group of parents described above at least roughly senses. These parents' emotional well-being, in fundamental ways, depends on their children's sports performance. "It would break my father's heart," a sixteen-year-old told me bluntly, "if I stopped playing hockey." It's not uncommon, research indicates, for children to continue to play sports to please their parents even though they've stopped enjoying it. In the book *Friday Night Lights* (which became a television show and film), about a Texas town intoxicated with high school football, athletes prop up not only their parents—many community members' well-being rises and falls on the team's performance. "Life really wouldn't be worth livin' if you didn't have a high school football team to support," a local realtor casually remarks.

And, like children whose parents are too hyped up about academic achievement, the children of these parents can suffer a fragile, diminished sense of self that impairs their capacity for caring and healthy relationships—they can learn to closet feelings such as fear or self-doubt that might be seen as impeding performance, and they can become unsure of what is valuable about themselves that is unrelated to their athletic performance. These children are also highly prone to shame when they believe that they have performed poorly, are more likely to view other children as competitors and threats, and can feel the corrosive weight of their parents' happiness on their shoulders, undercutting their parents as mentors. How can we as parents and coaches deal with our feelings so that they don't negatively affect our children's moral and emotional well-being?

It can help a great deal if we as parents and coaches can, first, reflect on why we stake so much on these events and are so easily provoked. Many of us are far too wrapped up in sports for the same reasons that we are caught up in our children's academic performance—our hopes that our children will compensate for our shortcomings, our belief that our children's performance signals our success or failure as parents, our status concerns and competitive feelings with other parents, the largely unconscious belief, engraved in our childhoods, that excelling is the only way to obtain love. Other parents get too caught up in these events because they know that sports achievements can give their child an edge in college admissions, and some parents simply take signals about the importance of these events from other parents—parents can jack each other up.

But there are also particular reasons that sports are especially compelling to us as adults and can even become the center of our lives. For adults who experience their lives as featureless and monotonous, children's sports can provide a thick plot, a varied narrative that is far more compelling than that of college or professional sports because their own child is a central character. For other adults, the rhythms of winning and losing in sports—the cycles of disappointment and success—are simpler and ultimately more gratifying than the rhythms of conflict and uncertainty in their own lives. Adults with chronic job worries, for example, can pin their hopes instead on the uncertain but more predictable cycles of winning and losing in high school football games, can use these sporting events to regulate their moods—a tacit subject of *Friday Night Lights.*

Others of us are deeply invested in our children's sports because we see sports as a way of creating a deep bond with our children and as a test of whether our child is fundamentally like—or unlike—us. As the narrator observes in Tom Perrotta's acclaimed short story, "The Smile on Happy Chang's Face," "Like most men, I'd wanted a son who reminded me of myself as a kid, a boy who lived for sports, collected baseball cards, and hung pennants on his bedroom walls." The narrator's grief that his son is so different from him in this respect is so great that it is responsible in part for this father assaulting his son, an act of violence that rends this father from his family.

Finally, children's sports can stir up in us old childhood wounds and yank us back to old childhood battles—struggles with shyness and self-assertion, peer and sibling rivalries, difficulties with authority, painful experiences of unfairness and mistreatment. I have seen parents become enraged when they think that their child has been treated unfairly—anger that seems far out of proportion relative to the event. As one self-aware father put it: "My kid wasn't getting enough playing time, and I found myself furious at his coach. I couldn't leave it. I had reason to be angry, but not *that* angry. I'm not sure where that was coming from."

It's useful for us as parents to have at least some understanding of these underlying psychological dynamics. But even when we are not prone to looking inward in these ways, many of us have some awareness of our overinvestment—that's why the audience members described above laughed knowingly in response to the father's confession. There are moments during children's sporting events when we are provided telltale signs of our overinvestment, moments when we find ourselves invaded by a troubling feeling we can't quite push away, such as the father who realizes that he's too angry about his son's lack of playing time. I remember realizing that whether my child's hit slipped by the shortstop or was caught might affect my mood for days, and being furious at a perfectly innocent eight-year-old child who kept striking out my son and his teammates. In Perrotta's short story, the narrator, who is the umpire of a Little League game, wants one team to "humiliate" and mercilessly "taunt" the other team because the other team is coached by his neighbor, a bitter rival: "feelings you can't hide from yourself, even if you'd just as soon chop off your hand as admit them to anyone else." We might also catch ourselves in the gutter of sexist and racist stereotypes or casting aspersions on another team because they come from this or that community—a wealthy community easily characterized as snotty or a high-crime, poor one, say. The sports consultant Greg Dale coaches parents to be alert to other classic signs of their overinvestment, such as saying "we" won or lost the game, regularly occupying dinner conversations with talk about children' sports, and planning family vacations around these events.

There are, too, ways that we as parents can get important feedback from others about our level of intensity and behavior. Dale suggests that parents ask their spouse and children whether they find their behavior embarrassing. One question in particular, Dale argues, is a kind of litmus test: "Are you reluctant to sit with me in the stands?" Luckily, some teenagers, perhaps the healthiest ones, have the gumption simply to tell their parents, as one seasoned coach puts it, "to buzz off." Yet we can also get feedback from our children about whether they want us to attend a game, about what we might do at games that would be helpful, and about when and how they want advice. (Most children don't want frequent advice, and they especially don't want advice right before or after a game.)

And when we find ourselves overinvested, we might consider, Dale suggests, taking a break, skipping a few games. We might also ask ourselves whether we have a gratifying life outside of sports.

As with academic achievement, it can be helpful to talk to children about our own history with sports and to be honest with children about our feelings. We certainly do *not* need to share with children all of our unreasonable hopes and conflicts about sports. But when we are visibly grim when our child performs poorly or loses a game, or when we find ourselves shrieking at a coach or referee, we should assure our children that this behavior is not a reflection of what we value at our most mature moments. Because we may signal our intensity to our children unconsciously and because children may misread our intentions, it can also help to articulate clearly what our best instincts tell us and to encourage children to let us know if they feel we are betraying our own principles. As one parent, concerned about what she might be communicating unconsciously, said to her children, "This is what is important to me — never, never play sports for me or for your dad. If that's why you're doing it, *stop*."

In the big picture, though, what may be most important is if we as parents help our children develop a healthy perspective on sports. Sometimes this means cultivating in children a sense of irony. I remember driving home with a friend, Paul, and our thirteen-year-old boys from their basketball game. The boys' team had lost, and we'd had to drive forty-five minutes to the game. Paul's son, Aaron, had sat on the bench the entire game. I was trying to assess what kind of mood Aaron was in, and how Paul was going to handle it. I was worried that both Aaron and Paul were fuming, and that Paul was feeling sorry for Aaron in a way that would only pour salt in Aaron's wounds. I was also worried that Aaron might quit the team.

Paul asked Aaron how he was doing, and Aaron had the poise to make a joke: "Hey, Dad, can I sit on the couch and watch television all week so I can prepare for sitting on the bench at the game next week?" Paul didn't miss a beat: "Maybe we can get you a bench and you can sit on it for your school talent show." Aaron had another idea: "And no exercise. Please don't let me get any exercise this week. I need to be able to sit at the game."

Parents and coaches should obviously not launch into jokes when a child has a disappointing experience. It's crucial here that Paul took Aaron's lead. Yet Paul is able to joke with Aaron this way because Paul does not see sports performance as a measure of Aaron's value. Paul later told me that he was quite proud that Aaron was able to joke about his sitting on the bench—it was to Paul a measure of Aaron's confidence and maturity, an indication of Aaron's ability to not get caught up in, and perhaps subtly critique, the inflated anxieties and angers that typically surround sports.

But I also know that Paul and Aaron are serious about sports. The humor works and provides some relief in this instance because it is connected to something that both Paul and Aaron take seriously. As much as many parents and coaches harp on sports being "just a game," our enjoyment from it comes from the fact that it is not, in fact, just a game—it's an arena, as Geertz observes, where we enact rituals with deep psychological meaning and deal with all sorts of inner conflicts. We don't have a vocabulary for describing this territory—perhaps what comes closest is theater—this space between real life and "games." It exists in a particular zone that has irony at its center: it works because it both means a great deal and doesn't mean anything at all. When the coach in the documentary film about girls' basketball, *The Heart of the Game,* exhorts his girls during a huddle with the chant, "Kill! Have fun!" he is expressing this irony. When Paul jokes with his son about sitting on the bench, he is expressing this irony as well. When parents treat sports as simply a game, they can rob children of sports' moral power. Conversely, when parents take sports as a true measure of their child's worth or capacities, or their worth, or their town's worth, they are not creating for children the opportunity to master conflict or develop understanding. They are introducing real conflicts that impair children's ability to value others and impede children's capacity for moral learning. They are turning sports into a false proving ground, setting children up for a pseudo sense of mastery, and undermining their role as moral mentors.

COACHES AND PARENTS

Early in *The Heart of the Game,* we see the players huddling intensely in the center of the court. They seem to exist in some separate universe. We hear their coach in voice-over, describing the core of his philosophy: "I dreamed up this idea that the team is the inner circle. And the purpose of the inner circle is to get the parents *out* of the team."

Just as is true with teachers and parents, positive relationships between parents and coaches can greatly benefit children's moral development. Coaches and parents can certainly be effective in instilling in children important values when their approaches to promoting character are similar and directly reinforce one another. Yet children can also benefit—when parents and coaches respect one another—from different approaches, as my children did with coaches who emphasized toughness.

Yet these days the parent-coach relationship is often troubled in many respects. Coaches, like teachers, often feel heavily scrutinized and patronized by parents whom they see as badly biased and as lacking the knowledge to judge them. Many coaches can reel off stories about parents who advocate fiercely for their own child without thinking for a second about what's good for other children or the team. Coaches can also resent parents who treat them as babysitters. "Some parents dump their kids with us. They just want their kids off their radar," is how one Little League coach puts it. On the other hand, almost all sports parents I know bristle about a coach who failed to appreciate or blatantly mistreated their child.

And these days the coach-parent relationship is troubled in another respect. While many schools have for decades actively encouraged at least some form of parent-teacher communication, the lines between parents and coaches have always been bright. While regular parent-teacher conferences are routine, I don't know any sports programs at any level that encourage routine parent-coach conferences. While for decades most teachers have been expected to be responsive to parents who ask about their practices and decisions, coaches have never in the past been expected to be transparent with parents about playing time and other key decisions. The coach is high priest; the court, rink, or field is his or her sanctum.

This divide is also great because coaches, especially serious high school coaches, are often trying to quickly create a sense of family on a team. Many coaches, like the coach in *The Heart of the Game*, worry that parents will disrupt team unity or quite explicitly see sports as a kind of oasis for children from the pressures of the outside world, including parental ones. The sports psychologist and consultant Jeff Beedy says that what most coaches want to say to parents is "Go home and mow the lawn."

Yet because we also live in an era when more and more parents are deeply invested in every aspect of their child's development and are micromanaging their children's lives, the potential for conflict is very high. For some parents in middle-class and affluent communities who expect to strongly influence other adults in their children's lives—teachers, babysitters, piano instructors—the closed culture of children's sports is maddening—and some of these parents are openly defying it. Further, while some parents are insistent and even threatening when they feel stonewalled by a coach, many of us as parents, bridling under communication restraints, may trespass these boundaries and attempt to manipulate coaches in far less obvious ways, ways that we may be only partly aware of. We might ask to assist coaches, for instance, knowing in the back of our minds that it may create opportunities to advocate for our kids. Or, like Jeff, we try to slip in a nugget of advice to coaches after and even before games (like teachers trying to prepare for class, coaches especially don't want parents' questions or input while they are engaged in last-minute game preparation). These parent-coach issues can be compounded by class differences. Research suggests that coaches with working-class roots, for example, are less likely to see these kinds of parental entitlement as the norm. Some coaches have grown up in communities where respect for a coach is assumed, not earned. This relationship can, then, quickly ignite. I have heard about communities where full-scale war breaks out, with parents rallying other parents and coaches closing ranks with other coaches.

There is much that can be done to prevent and help heal these rifts. It's important that coaches keep firmly in mind that mistreatment of children in sports is not rare—that parents have good reasons to be anxious about handing over responsibility of their child to a virtual stranger who, in the majority of informal leagues, has not been screened in any meaningful way. Coaches should recognize, too, that while there are advantages to creating a temporary space where children are insulated from family pressures, ultimately their job is not to rescue children from their families but to strengthen the tie between parent and child that is the backbone of moral development. That means that coaches should not only engage parents when a child is struggling, for example, but vigilantly avoid undermining parents and actively appreciate parents in ways that are visible to children. In more informal programs it is helpful to include parents at times in team events, such as getting pizza after a game.

Perhaps more important, though, parents' challenges to the traditional culture of sports can initiate a long-overdue conversation about what aspects of this culture should change. The nature of boundaries and the degree of exchange between coaches and parents should clearly depend on a child's age and the competitive level of a specific program. Yet there are examples of coaches who have constructively shifted these boundaries at every level, creating alliances with parents. I have seen coaches, for example, gather parents together after games to share with them what they said to their players about a victory or a defeat, describe the strengths and weaknesses of their team, explain their reasons for disciplining players, describe how they are seeking to motivate the team. Some coaches also define their values and describe to parents how they intend to nurture them in children. The sports consultants Jeff Beedy and Tom Zierk recommend that coaches in informal leagues send letters home to parents before the season, articulating their values and how they intend to promote them.

Further, coaches can both encourage parent involvement and clearly delineate what kinds of involvement are appropriate. Because coaches are commonly opaque about their beliefs and decisions, many parents, including large numbers of mothers who have never been immersed in a sports culture, have reasonable questions that go unanswered: Should I say something to a coach if my child is anxious or uneasy? Should I intervene if my child feels excluded or degraded by other members of the team? Should I speak to a coach if my child feels that she is playing the wrong position or believes that she is playing less than another player who is less skilled? Coaches can clarify that while it's not appropriate for parents to get involved in decisions about children's playing time relative to other players or team strategy, it is perfectly appropriate for them to talk to a coach, assuming their child feels it would be helpful, if their child feels anxious or excluded on the team. Dale recommends that coaches also designate a specific time during the week when it is appropriate for parents to voice their concerns.

And there is much that we as parents can do to strengthen this critical relationship. We should, for one, find a way to pause and reflect if we become infuriated with a coach. Dale recommends to parents the "twenty-four-hour rule." Before lashing out at a coach, "give yourself twenty-four hours to think it over." While it's important for us to be clear-eyed and discerning about a coach's strengths and weaknesses, we can also work to take coaches' perspective and to help our children take that perspective, including understanding what coaches have been asked to do and the conditions under which they have been asked to do it—in particular, that coaches are often inexperienced, that coaching, like teaching, requires a great array of complex skills and that few individuals possess all those skills, and that coaches are often volunteers with other major commitments. In choosing whether to talk to a coach, we should also ask ourselves what kind of precedents we are setting for other parents.

MORAL COACHING

Anyone who chooses to coach children has an image of what good coaching is. In the United States, chances are these images come from adults' childhood memories of their own coaches and from sports movies in the last few decades—*Hoosiers; Remember the Titans; Glory Road; Friday Night Lights; The Mighty Ducks; Coach Carter;* and *All the Right Moves,* among dozens of others. While images from these films are certainly more likely to resonate in communities that prize toughness, my guess is that they affect a wide range of coaches. I certainly had these movies in my head when I coached. The coaches in these films push children to excel and insist on absolute deference: "I am the law," Gene Hackman, playing the coach in *Hoosiers*, declares, "absolutely and without question." "This is no democracy," Denzel Washington's character states in *Remember the Titans*, "it is a dictatorship. [Once again] I am the law." Children are treated as misguided or as blank slates—they are relieved of the responsibility to think. Coaches tend to know little about players—coaches don't ask questions, they give orders—unless a crisis in a player's life intrudes on the team in some way.

At the same time, these coaches are deeply invested in their coaching—coaching consumes them—and they are willing to make great sacrifices for their players, often at least tacitly understanding that these boys need father figures. They are committed, as *New York Times* columnist David Brooks observes, to racial and social justice. They rally poor children on the edge of despair. Samuel L. Jackson's character tells his players in *Coach Carter* that they have "power beyond all measure." Denzel Washington's character insists that white players understand and respect black players, and vice versa.

In terms of children developing morality, there is much to commend these images. Children not only clearly need adults who push them and invest in them, but also adults who stand for racial and social justice.

Yet in crucial respects, this type of coaching is absolutely wrong for children and can be harmful to their moral development, especially because the great majority of children who play organized sports are young and play in informal leagues. Most kids start playing sports at about five years old; 70 percent of children quit organized sports by age thirteen. Coaches are often children's first mentors—for some children coaches will be their only mentors—and coaches can have a significant bearing on children's developmental trajectories. Yet, like other adults, coaches' effectiveness as moral mentors depends on their ability, unlike these film characters, to get to know individual children, to see themselves as in a reciprocal relationship with children, and to respect children's capacity to think. Perhaps most important, coaches can seize opportunities to develop children's capacity for moral reasoning and appreciation.

I remember getting a glimpse of how coaching could promote appreciation in children several years ago, when I was an assistant basketball coach in a league for eight- to eleven-year-old boys. In the middle of the season, as we were struggling to make the playoff, the league placed on our team a boy who had just arrived from Ethiopia and who had never played basketball before. In his first game he flung the ball all over the court, forgot to dribble, mangled every conceivable rule. Several of the players reacted as if a grenade had been thrown into their midst. Rather than ignoring or reinforcing his players' impulse to scapegoat this player, the head coach pulled aside a couple of boys who were having the hardest time with this newcomer and engaged them in this boy's perspective. "What do you think it's like to come to a new country? To play a game you haven't played before? To have people screaming at you in a language that you don't understand?"

When coaches of teams of younger kids not only insist on equal playing time for all children but explain why equal playing time is important, when they point out the strengths of weaker players in nonpatronizing ways or laud opposing players or the opposing coach, they similarly enhance children's capacity to appreciate others. The sports consultants Beedy and Zierk imagine the field or court as a kind of classroom. They encourage children to reflect, for example, on rituals that have become empty, such as the classic chant after games for the opposing team: "Two, four, six, eight, who do we appreciate?" As Zierk points out, "Children often don't have a clue what they're saying or why they're saying it, so I ask them, and we break it down. Why do we appreciate the other team? Is it because they played well? Because they played fairly? Because we would want to be appreciated?" (I spoke with a thirteen-year-old who told me: "For a long time I thought we were saying, 'Two, four, six, eight, who do we eliminate.'")

Coaches can enhance moral reasoning by helping children sort through their moral dilemmas in sports. These dilemmas pop up almost constantly. Should I tell a coach if a teammate is breaking a rule? Should I react aggressively to an opposing player who is aggressive? Should I encourage a teammate who is scoring a lot but who plays selfishly?

In children's sports there are also commonly transgressions rich with possibilities for developing appreciation and moral reasoning, but adults often treat these incidents like a live wire. As Beedy points out: "A parent makes a racist comment, or the coach of the opposing team says something sexist about a girl who is playing, and the kids plainly see it and hear it but no one ever talks about it."

I remember watching my son play in a basketball game that veered out of control—players were fouling each other hard, and the referee was making calls that seemed arbitrary. A parent from our team started yelling at the referee, "They're hurting our kids." At the end of the game our coach refused to shake the hand of a player on the other team, which caused three parents of the other team to bound out of the stands onto the floor. One of the parents bellowed at the coach: "You asshole, shake his hand. Don't treat our kids that way." The players froze, their jaws dropping in varying mixtures of fear, fascination, and excitement, all the adult character-education rhetoric suddenly detonating around them.

Yet at no time was this episode even raised with the players, let alone explored, by our coach or by a league official. It's an episode, though, that is both deeply troubling and a powerful springboard for thinking through common and complex moral issues and responsibilities: Is it ever appropriate to refuse to shake someone's hand after a game? What was this coach's perspective and how might this coach have responded constructively? How might parents have handled this situation constructively?

Beedy points out that coaches often overhear all kinds of conversations outside of the game itself, including conversations on the bus or driving children to and from games, that reveal "how players treat their girlfriends, who is using drugs, who's acting

crazy." Yet coaches seldom see these conversations as either opportunities for moral learning or interventions of any kind.

And coaches can be far more open not only with parents but
with children about their thinking and decisions. While many
coaches are transparent in these ways, others are needlessly un-
communicative with players at every level of children's sports, often depriving them of opportunities for moral learning and undermining their trust and respect. While here, too, there ought to
be clear understandings about what questions and concerns are
appropriate for players to raise, and when they should be raised, it
is commonly acceptable for coaches to leave children in the dark
when children feel they have been treated unfairly—when they've
been yanked out of a game suddenly, say—something we would
not accept from adults in other contexts.

And Beedy and Zierk go one step further. They argue that sports
for young children in informal leagues should be far more democratic—that children should have opportunities to co-construct
rules and to determine sanctions for violating them—and that
coaches should be far more Socratic in their communication with
players, drawing our their thinking. As with schools and other environments, children are more likely to internalize moral standards when they participate in their creation and are responsible
for enforcing them. While in pickup sports children regularly create, negotiate, and enforce rules, these opportunities have been
lost as more children have taken up organized sports. Zierk recalls
coaching a soccer team of six-year-olds who came up with team
rules like "be nice" and "no putdowns, just putups"—rules that
were then inscribed on the ball—as well as punishments for children violating these rules (which were much harsher than Zierk's
own proposed punishments).

Yet ultimately, the effectiveness of coaches, like teachers, hinges
on their getting to know individual players, seeing themselves as in
relationship with their players, and reflecting on how they are succeeding and failing as moral mentors. While many coaches clearly
do get to know and care a great deal about their players, many

coaches I know are quick to identify players' talents and weaknesses, but are remarkably incurious about the kind of people players are. I know coaches in informal leagues who never ask children their names and never encourage children to learn each other's names. Too often coaches never tune in to the particular circumstances of a child (like the Ethiopian boy). For coaches to be effective moral mentors they ought to know, at the very least, when a child is seeking a fun, social experience, for instance, and when a child wants to be aggressively pushed. Children and parents might fill out a brief survey where they spell out their hopes and concerns. At the same time, character-education programs and consultants need to give coaches a language for thinking and talking about their relationships with kids that doesn't smack of the therapeutic culture, a language that is not fuzzy and saturated with psychological jargon, but that instead describes in clear, plain terms the value of listening to and talking with children and provides concrete strategies for connecting with different types of children. These kinds of relationships, to be sure, will be hard to realize in the many circumstances where adults are roped into coaching without any mentoring or training and have little contact with children outside of actual games. Yet in every context these relationships are worth striving for.

Most fundamentally, Beedy and Zierk recommend that coaches figure out their own motives for coaching and be certain that their motives are of a sort to promote healthy relationships with children. As Zierk puts it, "Is it to get out of the house? To win? Are you living vicariously through these kids? Is it for fun? Was I unwillingly drafted? Coaches need to recognize what it is and deal with it." This kind of reflection is especially important because many children will constantly question and test whether coaches are really in it for themselves.

Finally, while it's important for parents and coaches to work on their attitudes and behavior, it's also important to change the rules and policies of many sports programs. For one, administrators of sports programs can do far more to establish constructive expectations and conventions. A contract pulled together by a large array of sports organizations in Massachusetts, for example, requires parents sign off on the following: "I will remember that children participate to have fun and that the game is for youth, not adults," "I will refrain from coaching my child or other players during games and practices, unless I am one of the official coaches of the team." "I will demand that my child treat other players, coaches, officials, and spectators with respect regardless of race, creed, color, sex, or ability." Many leagues are establishing concrete rules that prevent less talented children from being neglected, such as requiring, in leagues for children twelve years old and younger, that every child on a team play at least half the game. And some programs are usefully policing parents who can't curb their destructive behavior, including prohibiting parents who have repeatedly violated rules from attending sporting events. It's important that this kind of oversight become typical.

As parents, while we are often highly active in lobbying for our own children, we are typically passive when asking hard questions about whether a particular sports culture serves *all* children well. Rather than simply angling for our children to get the best coach, we could, for example, support administrators in recruiting high-quality coaches and insist that all coaches are screened and receive some rudimentary training on safety, listening to children, and leading democratically. Rather than letting certain parents berate their child or a coach, we can push league administrators to create and monitor expectations for parents. Rather than lobbying for our child to get on a team with strong players because it is likely to win, we can press league administrators to assure that teams are roughly equal and that the process of sorting children among teams is equitable and fair. Rather than complaining about unfair selection processes in team tryouts only when our child is not chosen, we can address an unfair process even if our child has made the cut. That kind of advocacy is a moral stance; it is one powerful way in which we transfer our best moral instincts to our children.

8

CULTIVATING MATURE IDEALISM
IN YOUNG PEOPLE

SO FAR IN THIS book I have focused primarily on the role of
parents and other adults in cultivating key moral qualities in children and adolescents. Yet moral development, as I have argued,
can occur throughout the life span, and our tendency to believe
that moral development is a childhood matter has caused us to
overlook a period of moral growth that may be just as important
as childhood and early adolescence in shaping our moral qualities
as adults—late adolescence and young adulthood. It is when young
people are in their late teens, twenties, and early thirties that they
are typically determining their responsibilities in love and work
relationships and sorting out what it means to be citizens. It is also
during this time that young people often transform their appreciation of others into convictions about and commitments to a better and more just world and determine what role they will—or
will not—play in improving the lives of others.

IT'S NOT HAPPENING IN COLLEGE

Yet the places where so many young adults spend their late teens
and early twenties—colleges and universities—do strikingly little
to help them cultivate this kind of idealism or sort out their role.

Increasingly, colleges, and especially elite colleges, are organized around launching students into lucrative, high-profile careers. There are, to be sure, many exceptions: the John Templeton Foundation has an honor roll of one hundred colleges that take seriously developing students' capacity for citizenship and social responsibility. Yet as Harvard University's former dean Harry Lewis puts it, while universities "affect horror" when students view college as a vehicle for financial success, they give students neither an alternative, coherent purpose for a college education nor any guidance on how to discover larger purposes. The social critic and columnist David Brooks observes that universities are focused on safety, rules, and achievement, not idealism: "You're on your own, Jack and Jill, go figure out what is true and just for yourselves." To the extent that universities are interested in developing idealism in young people, it is typically in providing a fairly small number of students with opportunities for leadership in community service—a kind of "varsity ethics squad," as one university president says. In our culture and on our campuses, youthful idealism is also sometimes trivialized—treated as a naive, fleeting stage— even though young people's visions during these years can frame the work of their entire lives and shape societies.

Further, healthy idealism often develops in careful, ongoing conversation with a mentor. Some colleges, especially small colleges, take mentoring very seriously. But many college students never connect with effective mentors who support them in being both realistic and idealistic, who help them develop a hardheaded view of the difficulties of change while scaffolding their hopes and convictions. Worse, far too many students' idealism is eroded in their interactions with faculty.

Whether colleges should play a large role in shaping young people's basic moral character is a complex matter. Students are young adults who should have many of the freedoms of other adults— there are limits to how much colleges can influence and regulate students' lives. And it's a huge endeavor for colleges to try to change students' basic moral constitution. Nor do all young people need to devote their lives—or even part of their lives—to idealistic endeavors.

Yet colleges should at least support young people's moral growth and provide them with a rich sense of their possible roles in contributing to others.

MENTORING FAILURE

Colleges can shape idealism through course work, community service, community-wide moral expectations and standards, the kinds of student relationships they foster—and perhaps especially through the mentoring relationships at the heart of idealism. Even when young people don't have extensive contact with a faculty member, their idealism is often energized by an inspiring professor. When that professor is responsive to their particular concerns, his or her influence can be multiplied many times. In more intensive mentoring relationships, young people can sort out what they owe others, what is just and unjust, what they should stand for, how they might have an impact. These mentoring attachments are sometimes intensified by the fact that many young people, as they become adults, become more critical of their parents—and sometimes of the ideals their parents represent—and are eager to tether themselves to adults whom they perceive as strong in a way they see their parents as weak. Erik Erikson calls these mentors in young adulthood "guardians of a final identity."

Yet after talking to students from various colleges over the years, I came to realize that opportunities to promote idealism are routinely squandered and that most students are deprived of effective mentoring relationships. Often, in fact, college students must battle to hold on to their hopes and ideals.

Take Maya, a lovely, soft-spoken college freshman who is interested in a career working to alleviate poverty in developing countries. She is concerned, though, about the financial sacrifice she will be making if she pursues this calling. She also worries that this career will disappoint her status-conscious parents. Her father wants her to become an engineer.

She speaks to a professor she respects about her struggle, and what he says sticks in her head: "He basically warned me that most people who try to help poor people in developing countries end up doing more harm than good. Then he rattled off a bunch of examples. I started to think: Maybe it's not worth it to try to change the world. Would I be wasting my life?"

Many students, like Maya, arrive at college or graduate school with large idealistic ambitions, whether it's curing major diseases, ending poverty, or reforming education. Yet they can quickly feel blizzarded in their classes with cold facts about highly touted, idealistic initiatives that come crashing against reality. One of the most common complaints of my graduate students is that their courses greatly hone their ability to view critically—to trash—seemingly valuable initiatives, but do little to cultivate in them a sense of possibility. In the 1980s and 1990s, two courses at Harvard University—a course on social reflection and activism taught by Robert Coles and a course taught by Brian Palmer on how students can make a difference as global citizens—were immensely popular in no small measure because they dealt directly with how ardent social leaders persevere in the face of hard challenges. Far too many universities have dangerously abandoned instilling hope as a core aspect of their mission.

College mentors can fail to nurture idealism in young people in several crucial, specific ways. Young people like Maya are often "trying out" idealism, dipping their toes into the waters of a certain kind of life, and they need practical help in determining not only what kind of financial sacrifice they will be making if they take up a cause, but how they will balance work and family obligations, and if they will be respected by people they respect. Some young people need help avoiding what's trendy and finding out what is likely to be most meaningful to them over the long term. "Idealism has become commercialized," is how one student puts it. "People jump on the latest bandwagon, whether it's AIDS in Africa or Darfur."

Other young people need to accept their many mixed motives for pursuing ideals. Sometimes young people steer away from idealism because they come to feel that a need to feel virtuous or a need for recognition—not pure altruism—is motivating their idealism. "The terrible burden idealism has to carry is that many people believe it either has to be pure or else it is worthless," the psychiatrist and author Eli Newberger points out. Some young people are acutely aware that college and graduate school admissions pressure have created a kind of community-service Olympics, generating all kinds of false or souped-up idealism: "At my school you can't just give flowers to sick people or the elderly," is how one high school student puts it. "You have to wipe out AIDS in Africa." Yet young people rarely have mentors who can help them disentangle these knotted motivations.

Perhaps most concerning, large numbers of young people experience significant disappointment and disillusionment in their idealistic pursuits but don't have access to mentors who help them work through these feelings. Professors and parents commonly assume that a year abroad working in a developing country or a stint of community service at an urban school will strengthen young people's commitment to improving the world. But I have talked to many young people after these stints who have either faced problems they find intractable, become suspicious of the authority figures entrusted to deal with these problems, or confronted injustices that seemed impossible to remedy. I recently talked to a teacher, fresh out of graduate school, who landed in an utterly chaotic school where she felt physically threatened by one student, unsupported by the principal, and isolated from her colleagues. She had come to speak with me to elicit my ideas about other careers.

Finally, too often mentoring relationships themselves become troubled and fractured: students end up embittered and questioning the integrity of faculty members. The pervasiveness of this harm caught me off-guard while I was talking informally a few years ago to a group of graduate students I respect a great deal. I asked them whether they felt well mentored: "Hardly any professor is interested in mentoring here," Monica, a warm, bright student from Georgia, remarked. Another student, Gail, added: "When I first came here I thought professors would be thinking about me and my development, that these relationships wouldn't be cluttered with all the expectations of my parents. But then at some point you realize that your relationships with professors aren't uncluttered at all. Most of the time it's not really about you, or at least it's just as much about them." "Some professors make it seem that it's about you," William, an older student, clarified, "but usually it's also about advancing their career in some way. It's about reciprocity."

To be sure, the student-faculty relationship is complex, and some students have unrealistic expectations of faculty members, in part because they are looking to mentors for compensation for the failures of their parents: the possibilities are thus high that even minor slights, manipulations, or deceits will fracture these young people's trust, if not send them into a free fall. There are also clear differences between undergraduate and graduate life. While many graduate students like those I spoke with have difficulties with mentors, faculty members in graduate programs — especially professional schools — are more likely in general than undergraduate faculty to be engaged in mentoring. Many graduate program faculty at least have conversations with students about their careers, conversations in which students' possible roles in contributing to others may be discussed.

Yet especially in high-powered universities where faculty members' careers are heavily dependent on their research, many students get short shrift. Faculty seldom receive training or support in mentoring students; the capacity to mentor is typically not a significant factor in hiring or promotion and there are often no incentives for faculty to take the work of mentoring seriously. One faculty member I spoke with, a highly respected mentor, felt that mentoring is, in fact, unwittingly discouraged: "The incentives are perverse. My reward for mentoring is that I get to write more recommendations." There are also typically no means of providing periodic feedback to professors on their mentoring or of sanctioning them for failures. As a result, many faculty do fail to tune in to students or think of students primarily as resources for advancing their work.

That faculty members often fail in these ways certainly does not mean that young people in their orbit will become cynical. Yet especially when adults' unresponsiveness or cynicism is combined with other factors—when parents or mentors are also, in particular, piling on pressure to achieve—the chances that young people will devote a significant part of their lives to improving the lot of others become small.

What can colleges and universities do to nurture healthy idealism? Minimally, a track record of mentoring should be one factor in hiring and promotion of faculty, and incentives and support should be provided for those faculty who are deeply invested in mentoring (that support might take the form, for example, of freeing these faculty from other academic obligations). Far more attention can also be paid both to providing courses across a wide range of disciplines that offer images of roles and careers that address pressing problems and to closely tying this course work to carefully structured and supervised community-service opportunities. Some college presidents have also explicitly set out to cultivate social responsibility. Led by its president, Tulane University, for example, has organized itself around the post–Hurricane Katrina rehabilitation of New Orleans and has created many opportunities for students to take part in this effort.

CULTIVATING HOPE

There is also much that parents and other mentors can do to promote mature idealism in young people and to shepherd them through disillusionment. As parents we can ask ourselves whether we are creating conditions in our homes in which idealism can take root—whether we are regularly bringing to our older children's attention problems in the world, exploring with children the many ways they can respond to these problems, and routinely providing children with stories that can help them imagine a life built on their convictions—something that in nonreligious communities parents seldom do. We can ask, too, whether we are giving serious time ourselves to improving the lives of others on any significant scale, or at least modeling engaged citizenship. Research reveals that children will often imitate their parents' specific acts of citizenship and commitment. One of the strongest predictors of voting are young adults' memories of their parents voting, discussions with parents about elections, and accompanying parents to the polls.

As parents and mentors we can, too, validate the complex array of motives that often propel idealism and other moral actions, including a need for recognition, envy, and guilt. We should consider sharing how our own ambitions and self-concerns are laced together with our altruism and compassion. For example, I sometimes ask students I'm advising about careers how important receiving recognition for their work and having a large influence are to them, and I'm honest with them that these things have been factors in my career choices.

Perhaps most important, as parents and mentors we need to help young people work through their disillusionment as they come to learn more about the world in all its stubborn complexity, so that they don't swing from wide-eyed idealism to dark pessimism. Part of what makes this challenge difficult is that so little is known about disillusionment. While we have an extensive language for talking about problems like grief and depression—and the varieties of these troubles have been finely recorded—we hardly have a vocabulary for talking about the many forms of disillusionment, including the pain one experiences as one uncovers injustice or seemingly insoluble problems in the world.

There are some practical guideposts, though, that can help us in this task. It's important that we introduce young people gradually to hard realities, leaven our stories of failure with examples of success, and provide examples of young people themselves who have taken fresh, useful approaches to entrenched problems. It's important that we take the time to understand very specifically where young people feel stuck, let down, or betrayed and that we help them sort out to what extent those disappointments and betrayals are a function of unreasonable expectations and to what extent they reflect realities that ought to and can be changed. Young people who become disillusioned with political or community leaders who make compromises need to know, for example, that compromise is often *not* the enemy of idealism: compromise is often a way of engaging the diverse stakeholders needed to sustain change over time. It's also important that we are sensitive to the nuances of our relationships with young people, tuning in specifically to how they might, reasonably or unreasonably, feel betrayed or disappointed by us. Because young people these days can be remarkably conformist—as Brooks observes, this generation of young people is "not trying to buck the system; they're trying to climb it"—we can also, in helping them re-create their ideals, encourage them to question and to perhaps depart from prevailing views.

At the same time, it's crucial for us as parents and mentors to be certain that our own disillusionments are not undermining young people's idealism—and our conversations with young people provide us with a powerful opportunity to revisit the state of our ideals. Over the last several years I have talked to many parents who are discouraged, if not altogether jaded, about efforts to improve the world on any large scale. These parents have not simply thrown up their hands. But they have come to question their own capacity—and often their children's capacity—to make a difference, and they worry that their botched-up, confused feelings do little to inspire their children. As one mother put it: "Some days I think I model healthy idealism for my children. But most days I think the world is intractable. I've spent years working on global warming, and I don't know that I've made any headway. My kids asked me the other day whether I thought people would survive until the end of this century, and I couldn't honestly say 'yes.' Often I think I'm a rotten influence on my kids."

In the end, our success as parents and mentors may depend on our capacity to work through our own disillusionment. This working-through is not only for our children's sake—our mature idealism can be a crucial source of vitality and a powerful force in the world. For some of us, that will mean taking on a certain derogation we experience or imagine, a sense that idealism is viewed as adolescent. For others of us, it will mean asking hard questions about the true nature of our idealism. While many baby-boomer parents wax nostalgic and congratulate themselves about their lofty '60s ideals and lament their children's lack of idealism, many of these parents never had strong and resilient ideals to begin with—the real idealism of the '60s provided cover for all sorts of pseudo, trendy idealism.

Yet most commonly it will mean reflection, and talk with each other, about where we got stuck and how we can get unstuck. And in this reflection and talk we can model for our children that idealism at whatever scale is not a feel-good exercise, a ride in a moral theme park, but a demanding and rigorous, as well as richly gratifying, way of leading one aspect of our lives.

All this is possible. But it will require for many of us as parents and mentors a sea change. It will mean that we neither wipe our hands of responsibility for children's moral fate as they enter early adulthood nor seek to micromanage their decisions. Instead, here, too, we will need to engage in the complex choreography of leading and following, helping them uncover their passions and listening to what weighs on their decisions while bringing to bear our wisdom. It will also mean that we as parents carefully examine our priorities in guiding our children about colleges, factoring in whether colleges really care about young people's character or seek to inspire idealism. It will be a good day when admissions officers are bombarded with questions not about the weight given to SATs in admissions but about how a university or college defines character and idealism and goes about cultivating them in students.

Moral development is lifelong. So is the task of parenting a moral child.

9

KEY MORAL STRENGTHS OF CHILDREN ACROSS RACE AND CULTURE

I HAVE EXPLORED in this book many reasons why adults succeed and fail as moral mentors. Yet this kind of analysis masks a
fundamental truth: there are great differences in parenting practices, as well as in the obstacles children face to becoming good
people, across race, economic class, ethnicity, and culture. These
differences are no small matter; they generate in children different
moral weaknesses and strengths, mold how children think about
moral problems, influence the critical emotions underlying morality, and shape how moral qualities are expressed. These differences in parenting practices and outcomes are important to understand because our country is becoming diverse at an astonishing
pace and because our children are who we are as a country. But
they are also vital to understand because for too long we have tried
to apply the same solutions, the same generic prescriptions, to
markedly different problems. Because of varying parenting and
community beliefs and practices and varying community strengths
and adversities, the challenges and the pathways to becoming a
good person are simply not the same in the white, tony suburbs of
New York as they are in the middle-class black neighborhoods of
Atlanta or the Mexican barrios of Los Angeles. We need to think
about how to help children become moral people in these very
different circumstances.

And it is vital that we understand these differences for another reason. Popular images and stereotypes have obscured for many Americans the strong or exemplary moral qualities of many poor children and of immigrant and African American children across economic class. While many of these qualities are obvious to African Americans and to immigrants themselves, they have gone unrecognized by other Americans. I am not glossing over troubling trends in low-income black and Latino communities, including the large numbers of black and Latino young people who are now in jail. Yet contrary to these stereotypes, there is much that parents across race, ethnicity, and class can learn from each other about raising moral children.

It is clearly beyond the scope of this book to explore these different obstacles and strengths across the vast array of economic and cultural groups that now comprise America. Nor will this chapter explore key differences within economic, racial, and ethnic groups that are rooted in regional values, rural-urban differences, and religious affiliation, among many other factors. What I do seek to address here are some of the most troubling stereotypes and a few key questions: What are some of the central differences in the challenges and pathways to becoming a good person across race, class, and ethnicity? What are some of the key, impressive moral strengths of immigrant and African American children and what parenting and community practices are responsible for generating those strengths? What lessons can be learned from these parenting practices?

THE MORAL EXPERIENCES OF IMMIGRANT CHILDREN

"It's totally predictable," Sam Michaels, a recently retired school principal said to me. "Immigrant kids would come to our school, and they'd be as sweet and respectful as they could be. Yet my whole staff would get this sinking feeling. We'd see exactly where these kids were heading, that pretty soon they'd have all the attitude of American kids."

Americans' fears about rising waves of immigrant children (about one in five children now live in an immigrant family, and that percentage is increasing at a rapid rate) run flat in the face of an astonishing fact. Even though large numbers of immigrants arrive impoverished, first-generation immigrant children, across almost every immigrant group, are, on average, faring better than their American-born counterparts on almost every school, health, mental health, and moral measure. While there is clearly huge variation in children's experience here, these children are in general less likely to be delinquent, to suffer behavioral problems, to abuse drugs, and to suffer the kinds of emotional troubles that impede healthy, caring relationships. I have talked to other adults who, like Sam Michaels, describe newly arrived immigrant children in glowing terms—as sweet, engaging, open, respectful.

That's the bright side of the story. The dark side is quite shocking. Many immigrant children, to be sure, fare extremely well in this country over time, and their fates have a great deal to do, among many factors, with what kind of communities they land in. Yet on average, the longer immigrant children live in this country, across almost all immigrant groups, the worse are the indications of their health, their school performance, and their moral functioning. A stark fact is that as English proficiency grows, school performance drops: the two are *inversely* related. The longer immigrant children are here, it appears, the more likely they are to disrespect adults and engage in troubling behaviors, such as substance abuse and delinquency. Marcelo Suárez-Orozco, a New York University researcher who, along with his wife, Carola, has conducted a major study of immigrant children, observes that many newly arrived immigrant children "talk about how beautiful school is and how wonderful the principal is." What do they say a few years later? "School's boring and the principal is an idiot."

Worse still, with each generation, these destructive attitudes and actions become more common, so that third-generation immigrant children's rates of most of these behaviors are similar to those of U.S.-born white teens. Both Mexican and Asian children, by far the two largest immigrant groups (Mexico sends by far the most children; it is followed by the Philippines, China, and India), are, on average, hurt by Americanization. Immigrant families are not a threat to America's moral culture, as some conservatives suggest. On the contrary: America is a threat to immigrant children's moral development.

The bright beginnings of immigrant children in this country reveal a good deal about parenting practices that effectively cultivate key moral qualities. Across a wide array of immigrant groups —but especially in many Asian and Latino communities—research suggests that parents are commonly successful in part because they have largely avoided the problems of many American parents. These parents are less likely than white middle- and upper-class parents to treat their children as fragile, and they are more comfortable asserting authority, demanding respect, and holding their children to high moral standards. They are less likely to confuse being an authority with being a friend. Many times I have heard immigrant parents express shock and dismay about lax American parents and their feeble discipline efforts. "Here Americans are afraid to punish their kids," a Haitian father tells me. "That's why American kids are disrespectful. We don't understand it."

Immigrant children may also from early ages be less focused on their own needs than are their nonimmigrant counterparts. To say that Asian and Latino cultures, as is now often claimed, are "collective" while American culture is "individualistic" is, to be sure, too simple. New research reveals that many Asian and Latino parents are quite focused on certain forms of individualism in their children and that the degree to which parents emphasize obligations to others versus individualism varies depending on a child's developmental stage and on the social setting. Many immigrant

parents are highly focused on individual achievement. Nevertheless, research on Asian American and Latin American families
from several countries suggests that these children are more likely
than their peers to give priority to the needs of the family, to
downplay their own needs and desires if they conflict with the
family, to make sacrifices for the family, and to directly support
the family by helping with household maintenance and caring for
family members. Thus, while most Asian and Latino parents promote many forms of individuality and self-sufficiency, this individuality commonly exists in healthy tension with a strong sense
of responsibility for others. As social critic David Brooks observes,
immigrant families are "the antidote to the excessive individualism that social conservatives decry."

Many immigrant children's communities and schools reinforce
this attention to others. Large numbers of immigrant children
become skilled at understanding the perspectives of diverse children and adults because they have lived in multiple worlds from
early ages, jumping back and forth between mainstream white
worlds and their own communities of color. Carlos, a tall, handsome Dominican tenth grader, lives in a poor community but has
worked in affluent communities tutoring suburban children. I
have seen him in both environments, and he has tremendous ease
and grace in both of these worlds. It's not hard to believe that he
will realize his ambition to become a mayor one day. Danielle, a
Haitian child, is perceived as a moral leader in her diverse school
by both her teachers and peers in part because she takes various
perspectives and is keenly sensitive to marginalized students. She
is also adept at helping others without patronizing them—she
mothers other children without their feeling mothered.

These bright beginnings and these strengths of immigrant families contain important parenting lessons. When a community of
parents is on the same page, championing the same high standards, organizing their children around others, placing a high premium on collective responsibility and commitment to others

—while encouraging children to engage those outside the community—the moral benefits to children can be great. I'll have more to say about how other American families might learn from these benefits and strengths later in this chapter.

THE DOWNWARD SLIDE

The downward slide of immigrant children as they assimilate into the mainstream culture reveals a good deal both about immigrant parents' strengths and about the specific challenges immigrant parents face in raising moral children. This slide has been blamed on that classic villain—children's peer cultures. During their first years here, immigrant children, it is said, anxious for acceptance, begin to take on all the school-scorning, adult-bashing, trendy disillusionment of nonimmigrant American teenagers.

Yet as influential as peer groups can be, this decline may be more a story about the erosion of the relationship that is, once again, the most important to children's moral development—the relationship between parents and children.

I first became aware of some of the causes of immigrant children's difficulties several years ago when I received a call from a friend who is a Boston police officer. He was concerned about several Vietnamese teens who had run away from home. We decided to consult a Vietnamese community organizer as a first step, and she suggested that we conduct a focus group with Vietnamese parents.

During the focus group, the same themes kept emerging. Parents feared that their children were learning a lack of respect for authority from other children and from American culture. Some parents said that their children were becoming seduced by all the freedoms they had in this country and were neglecting home responsibilities. Like many other immigrant parents, these parents felt that when it came to discipline, their hands were tied, that the kind of corporal punishment in particular that was customary in their country for generations was forbidden here and might even cause a government agency to take their child away (and taking this kind of punishment away, as I take up later, is not simple).

Soon afterward I spoke with a Vietnamese college student, Anne, and she described these rifts from a different angle. She spoke of the great pull she felt from a young age to "fit in" with U.S.-born friends and the steady, acute sense of both confusion and "betrayal" that accompanied that pull. "You feel this great pressure to become an American. But you're also conflicted about it. You feel like you're mimicking like crazy but that you may never get being an American right. You acculturate and then you back-pedal as fast as you can. You're ashamed of your parents for not understanding American customs and being unrefined in certain ways, but then you're ashamed of being ashamed. You want to be an American, but then Americans ask you questions—many Americans have asked me whether Vietnamese people eat dogs—that make you wonder whether you *do* want to be an American. And then you think, what do I owe the country my family is from? Maybe everything. Maybe nothing. And then there's the lying. I lied to my parents constantly in high school because they wouldn't've approved of what I was doing—especially seeing boys. Lying also, I think, gave me some space to figure out who I wanted to be."

Runaways in immigrant families are certainly not typical, and there is huge variation in immigrant parents' relationships with their children depending on many family, school, community, and cultural factors. Yet research reveals that these parent-child fractures affect a wide array of immigrant families and that over time many immigrant parents lose their authority as moral mentors. In many contexts, immigrant children feel the need to distance themselves from their parents—or constantly feel pulled between their parents and peers—because they think that their parents have lit-

tle understanding of American culture and that their parents es-
pouse values or promote habits that will directly hinder their own
ability to form an American identity and to be accepted in America. When children embrace American notions of individualism
and self-esteem, they can collide with parents—many parents
worry that their children are becoming selfish. Like the Vietnamese student quoted above, many children struggle with a muddle
of contradictory feelings about their parents that include embarrassment, and children may find themselves lying to their parents
frequently in order to be accepted by their peers or to establish an
American identity. Some children feel forced to choose between
their parents' values and American values and between parents
and friends. Some choose their friends.

Other factors can fray this relationship and undermine parents
as mentors. Many immigrant children become ashamed of their
parents for getting stuck in low-status, dead-end service jobs. "A
lot of immigrant kids see what their parents do for work and think
their parents are chumps," says the sociologist Mary Waters. While
immigrant parents often feel proud of their jobs and income compared to their peers in their countries of origin, over time many
immigrant parents have a hard time protesting their children's
denigrating assessments of them. "When immigrant parents first
get here they are often happy with their jobs and think they are
making good money," Waters adds. "But they soon realize that
they're making little compared to other Americans and they feel
like they've been had." Making matters worse, over time many
first-generation immigrant families drift from relatives and tight-
knit immigrant communities into more anonymous neighborhoods, eroding parents' sources of support—further weakening
their capacities as mentors—and diluting communal messages to
children.

Second- and third-generation parents may lose their capacity as
moral mentors in another sense. These parents may be less likely
than first-generation parents to communicate basic hope to their
children—researchers speak of first-generation immigrants' "opti-

mism"—and children without hope are far more vulnerable to destructive peer groups and destructive activities of many kinds. Many first-generation parents, of course, have high hopes for their children even when they lose hope for themselves—that's why they work themselves to the bone. But as many parents in each subsequent generation find themselves in the same low-status jobs that dragged down their parents—researchers now speak of a rainbow underclass—this kind of hope, too, may drip away.

Immigrant parents, then, face especially muddy, complex challenges in raising moral children. For many immigrant parents, finding new, constructive means of discipline is a challenge. This country shouldn't tolerate corporal punishment. But it's no simple matter to replace discipline methods that have been used to raise children for hundreds if not thousands of years. What's more, in many circumstances when parents assert their values too aggressively, children can be pulled away from them, and parents must deal with the reality that children's need to form an American identity can trump their values.

The challenge for immigrant parents, then, is both the same as and quite different from that of most other American parents. Like other American parents, immigrant parents must understand their children's worlds, coordinate their children's perspectives and their own, and be able to take a third-person perspective, including taking a hard look at how their own history and their own parents' practices should inform and guide—but also might misinform and misguide—their own parenting. Yet immigrant parents have a particular high-wire act to perform. Their challenge, as Marcelo and Carola Suárez-Orozco suggest, is to maintain strong family ties and anchor their children in their cultures of origin in part to counterbalance both racism and the worst aspects of American individualism and hedonism—but also to loosen the reins and to help their children develop "bicultural competencies," the ability to move fluidly between their own and American culture, so their children don't have to make a stark choice between their parents' and their peers' values.

And there is much to be learned from immigrant parents. There is a critical message for American parents in immigrant parents' struggles with their children over their identity and character. Immigrant parents, it appears, are less likely than most other American parents to view their primary parenting task as assuring that their children are happy from moment to moment. They are more likely, instead, to see their main mission as moral, as assuring in particular that their children respect others, and they are willing to endure painful fractures with their children in the service of that goal. As a principal of a Boston school who lives and works in a community with many immigrant families recently said to me: "The immigrant parents I know, mostly Haitian and Vietnamese, care deeply about protecting their children's moral core. They're more likely to fight with their kids than other parents because they have this moral mission." There is courage in that, courage that might embolden us all.

THE MORAL EXPERIENCES OF AFRICAN AMERICAN CHILDREN

When many nonblack Americans think of black children, they imagine marauding teenagers caught up in gangs, or incarcerated, or other images of moral troubles. These stereotypes blot out both the great diversity in the experience of black children and the many impressive moral strengths of these children, their families, and their communities.

These strengths are suggested by children themselves. We asked children across race, class, and ethnicity in integrated settings what they admired—and did not admire—about both white children and black children. Nonblack children certainly described negative characteristics of black children (and black children were sometimes harsher than nonblack children in critiquing themselves). Yet we also found that many nonblack children described black children—and black children sometimes described themselves—as, singularly or in some combination of these qualities, more honest, less hypocritical, more independent-minded, more willing to assert their views, and less concerned about popularity than about respect in comparison with their peers. "[Black kids] are not afraid to speak their mind and they talk to anyone without caring about their race." "Black kids don't care about being stereotypically popular—they just say their opinion." "[Black kids] seem more independent and strong-minded." Several adults we spoke with who had worked in both black and white communities described similar strengths among black students. "Black kids here will tell the truth even if it costs them," is how one teacher puts it. "They aren't sneaky here the way they were in my suburban high school. They're more straightforward." Some black and white students also described black students as experiencing "more joy" in each other (although black students also criticized other black students for at times "tearing each other down"). "Black kids usually feel happy when someone else does well and they show it. They make you feel good even without knowing you." Many white students in a southern high school, interviewed by moral development scholar Mary Casey, similarly described black students as less hypocritical and as more able to find joy in one another.

Several years ago, as part of a graduate class I taught at Harvard on school reform, my students and I watched Frederick Wiseman's documentary film *High School II*. Early in the film an assistant principal is talking to a mother and her son, who appears to have been adrift at school and resistant to his teachers. Abruptly, the assistant principal suggests what he thinks the real problem is, that this student, who is black, does not like going to a school with so many white staff. The boy agrees, unsettling his mother. She says that he has to learn to relate to all kinds of people, no matter their skin color. When he has prejudices against some people or is angry, he has to learn to "use his feelings."

I asked my students, mostly white, what their reactions were to this scene, and most of the students expressed their relief that the assistant principal had taken a tough issue head-on. Then I saw Valora, an African American student, raise her hand and gather herself: "Of course it's not easy for black students to go to school with white teachers. But why does the assistant principal presume that is the main reason the student is having trouble in school? Lots of black kids go to school with almost all white teachers but most don't create trouble. There could be all kinds of other things going on with him that are giving him trouble. Why do white people so often think it's about them?"

At some point in childhood most black children must contend with what the African American scholar Janie Ward describes as a kind of a dual reality, what W. E. B. Du Bois called "double consciousness." They must understand the terms and perspectives of black culture—black reality, a kind of bulwark against the claims of white reality—while also seeing the world as white people see it. Often black children are growing up in an ethnically diverse environment where, like immigrant children, they come to understand the perspectives and reality of children from many cultures. To function in society, black children must become skilled at "reading" nonblack children and adults, at taking their perspective.

At the same time, black children must come to terms with the fact that white children and adults, like the assistant principal described above—as well as most of the students in my class and myself—commonly don't recognize that they are defining reality and that there are other realities. Ralph Ellison's famous novel *Invisible Man* deals with the rage of being unseen with which blacks have long had to contend, and blacks' knowledge that whites are unaware that they are unaware. Black children like Valora must often deal, too, with white adults who fail to see the way in which their definitions are offensive—white adults who have conceptions of reality, like the assistant principal, that are, for example, too simple and egocentric. Similarly, many white students pride themselves on being colorblind. These students fail both to see inequality and to understand how important an understanding of the meaning of race is for black children's identity and ability to navigate in the world—for black adolescents to understand how race affects how they are perceived, how they have been parented, and how race is connected to the cultural norms that frame their experience day to day.

In the face of these tests, black children can clearly fall into destructive forms of victimization, withdrawal, or rage. Yet to learn to deal with the subtle blindnesses, as well as the outright prejudices of others, other black children learn to manage feelings of inferiority, cynicism, and anger, including sometimes learning to "use their feelings," as the mother above puts it, in ways that are foreign to most white students. These coping strategies may be one reason that black children's self-esteem, research reveals, is as high or higher than white students'. Many children, like Valora, also develop a nuanced understanding about when and how to listen and learn and when and how to resist. It requires yet another level of self-discipline and compassion for a child or young person like Valora to care about white children and adults despite their blindnesses and flaws, to find humanity in those who misunderstand them, to develop some sense of appreciation for those who don't appreciate them or fathom their reality. It was this high standard that Martin Luther King Jr. sought to establish, of course, when he implored black Americans not to succumb to the bitterness of injustice, to love in the face of injustice, to be, in fact, "extremists for love."

There are many complex sources of these strengths—these strengths have deep cultural and religious roots—yet parents clearly play a powerful role, and not just in teaching black children to "use" or manage their feelings. Many African American parents place a high premium on decency and respect, and studies suggest that black children are more likely than their white peers to defer to their parents and other authorities. A few black children we spoke with who had spent time in suburban white communities were aghast at how impudently white children spoke to their parents: "If I spoke to my mother like that, I'd be kicked from here until I was forty." Some black parents convey quite explicitly that their children have to go out of their way to be responsible and respectful to defy pervasive racist images: "My parents tell me I have to do much better than the stereotypes," is how one tenth grader put it. The parenting weaknesses that often undermine appreciation and the development of the self in white, middle- and upper-class communities—treating children as fragile or as friends, satiating every need—are not major problems in African American communities. Research indicates that black families often emphasize perseverance in the face of adversity—an emphasis that is often strongly bolstered by deep religious beliefs—and are often forceful and "no-nonsense" with their kids while also communicating warmth in many ways. Delores Holmes, an African American educator who has worked for over thirty years with black families, also observes that black parents don't inundate their children with praise: "Black families communicate instead that good behavior, helping others in the family or the neighborhood, is expected, it's what you do. That's how kids develop ownership. That's how kids come to see these things as their responsibility." At the same time, black families often value both group effort toward common goals and, like immigrant families, interdependence and respect for family.

One reason that many black children may be more honest and direct than their typical white peers is because adults tend to be more honest and direct with them. Black scholars observe that black parents and teachers often confront children with hard realities because they worry that misbehavior could imperil these children's safety. Many black children may feel "more joy" in one another in part because, unlike in many white communities, there are strong, long-standing cultural norms in black communities that prohibit pushing forward one's own child while neglecting the advancement of other children.

The sources of moral troubles in African American communities are, of course, layered and intricate, and race and poverty often mix in complex ways. A few African American parents we spoke with expressed concern about boys' lack of emotional literacy and about parenting practices that have become outmoded. "Black parents used to have to dictate to their kids and discipline them all the time to keep them in check and to protect them from dangerous, racist white folks," is how one black parent put it. "That gets passed on from generation to generation—but it's not as necessary anymore and it's not helping our kids. Black parents need to listen to their kids more and kids need to learn to talk about their emotions." Will McMullen, a black psychologist who has worked with black families for many years, is concerned, in addition, about the tendency among some black parents to label their children as "bad" early in their lives and to tell them directly that they are "bad children." At the center of the troubles of children in poor black communities are, too, many of the same factors that destructively mix in immigrant communities. Many low-income African American parents must endure the hopelessness of finding themselves in the same poverty that dragged down their parents, generation after generation. Like immigrant parents, many African American parents must choose between making a reasonable living and spending a reasonable amount of time with their children, and many work in jobs their children don't respect. High numbers of African American children are also growing up without their fathers.

Rather than simply pushing generic moral-development strategies, it's vital to assist black children in dealing with the particular obstacles they face in becoming moral people. For example, many low-income black parents, like other low-income parents, can benefit from support from schools and family support programs in helping their children deal with anger and in cultivating in their children basic hope, often despite their own disillusionment and hopelessness. Children can also feel hope when their parents are mobilized and are provided resources and opportunities to affect change in their communities. This country also needs effective strategies for strengthening fathers' ties to their children in African American communities and many other communities. I take up these family support programs and father engagement strategies in the final chapter.

And as with immigrant families, the experience of these families contains important lessons for other parents. It would help many other families, for instance, to emphasize perseverance in the face of adversity, to praise less and to communicate instead that good behavior is to be expected, to emphasize group goals as well as individual achievements, to guide children in developing a more nuanced understanding about when to listen and comply and when to resist, to help children appreciate others despite their flaws, and to place a higher premium on respect for authority.

Many of these positive parenting practices, it's important to observe, are common in some white, nonimmigrant communities. In certain respects, parenting in low-income and working-class white families, for example, appears to be similar to parenting in immigrant and African American communities. Research suggests that in these communities, many parents, for example, in contrast to more affluent white parents, place a high premium on maintaining their authority, praise less, and are more likely to expect good behavior.

There are many unrealized opportunities for white middle- and upper-class parents to learn from lower-income parents and from both immigrant and African American parents. Many white, financially comfortable parents have regular contact, for instance, with adults of color who are caregivers—childcare providers, teachers, babysitters—and who have strong skills as moral mentors. But these white parents are often not alert to these skills.

Further, white parents can seek to give their children the opportunity to experience, at least for a period of time, life as a minority or outsider—an experience most white children never have—so that they must think a good deal about how a majority group thinks and feels. These experiences might include participating in an afterschool or sports program in which they are a minority.

These experiences are far less likely to be feel-good, token exercises if it is communicated to children that understanding how those from other cultures think and feel is a lifelong project, and if parents engage their children in reflecting on their own privileged position in the American mainstream in contrast to the experience of other American children. These parents can clearly also be conscious of choosing schools, afterschool programs, and neighborhoods with an eye toward diversity.

Just as important, white teachers and other adults working with black children commonly fail, as the education philosopher Audrey Thompson puts it, "to *see* the world that the children see." And while white children often know children of color who have sophisticated social knowledge and impressive moral qualities, adults seldom go beyond bland talk of multiculturalism, elevating and building on the social and moral strengths of diverse children. In many, perhaps most, places in the country, parents and teachers are still trying to teach children, in fact, simply to be colorblind. Rather than only seeking to mentor poor children and children of color so that they can adapt more effectively to white society, why not, for example, develop mentoring programs that reverse the usual arrangement, pairing teenagers and young adults of color with white elementary school children? Adults can also help children of color recognize their possibilities as moral leaders. Many African American and immigrant children do not yet see in themselves this potential; it's not a role they associate with themselves. It's time to think hard about how to build these children's capacity to be moral ambassadors in a diverse world and to realize their families' contribution to the nation's moral life.

CONCLUSION: MORAL COMMUNITIES

A FEW YEARS AGO I was walking several blocks from my house around eleven at night. As I turned a corner and entered a busy intersection, I saw several police cars, parked at angles and facing each other. The headlights of the cars converged on a teenage boy —slight, hunched over, his hands handcuffed behind his back, his head bent over slightly, his face registering very little.

I recognized him—I'll call him William—immediately. I had coached him in basketball a few years before, when he was twelve and thirteen years old, and he was one of my favorite players. He was affable, energetic, a little devilish in a way that was mostly innocent fun. He tuned in to adults quickly and was a generous teammate.

In retrospect, I'm not sure why seeing William in handcuffs took me off-guard and shook me so deeply. I had heard over the previous couple of years that he had been truant from school and had taken on a thuggish quality with his teachers. I also knew that he had been arrested a few times for robbery and drug use. I knew that William's father, a corporate executive often on the road, drank a great deal and could be harsh and critical with him, and that his mother seemed disconnected, withdrawn.

But this night the full force of his plunge hit me dead-on, partly, perhaps, because I felt some sense of responsibility. I felt that I had lost one of "our" kids. Over the following few days I spoke with a few other parents who were connected to William and his family and it was clear that they felt the same way.

I began thinking about what I might have done to change William's trajectory. What kind of conversation might I have had with either William's parents or his school counselor and at what point? What might have been the outcome of such a conversation? Why was my reflex, and the reflex of other parents who knew this family, to avoid that conversation?

* * *

Not long ago I spoke to Jerome Kagan, the legendary child psychologist and moral-development scholar, about the state of American children. Kagan has looked at how family practices have varied throughout history, and he has never been more concerned than he is today: "Children and parents internalize the values of their culture, and our culture has become more self-interested than it was in earlier generations. There is not a balance between responsibility for community and the self's desires for enhancement. Look at the heads of Enron, and priests abusing boys, and salespeople working for mortgage companies who, without shame or guilt, sold large mortgages to adults they knew could not make the payments. We have lost a national consensus on what comprises a conscience."

While I have focused in this book on the moral and mentoring capacities of parents, these capacities do not, of course, exist in a vacuum. Parents, teachers, and coaches, as well as children, are causes and products of the cultural trends of their times.

There are, to be sure, positive cultural trends—many more American parents, for instance, are teaching children to value diversity and are instilling in girls the belief that they have the same career options as boys. But there are also cultural characteristics and trends that are troubling. When Americans want something done well we almost invariably do it in teams, whether it's building a rocket, countering terrorism, or developing a new product. Yet when it comes to what is arguably the most important thing we do—raising moral children—American parents tend to be isolated and dangerously insulated from feedback of any kind. Research suggests that many parents are reluctant to interfere in the lives of other families even when they suspect a neighbor of abusing a child. That's one reason children like William slip through the cracks. At the same time, professionals working with families, not only teachers and coaches but many healthcare professionals, childcare workers, pastors, and many others, tend to treat parenting as private and are reluctant to confront parents when they are concerned about a child. Our political leaders have also been unwilling in many cases to challenge parents in appropriate ways. What makes this reluctance to challenge parents so concerning is that we as parents—as this book has tried to show—primarily jeopardize our children's moral development in ways that are outside our awareness.

Another cultural trend is also deeply troubling: many parents these days are simply self-interested and self-protective, in some cases abdicating fundamental moral responsibilities. Nowhere is this abdication more glaring than in the case of fathers. Fathers across race and class lines are abandoning their children in droves. Recall that large numbers of children born to unwed mothers and children of divorced parents lose contact with their fathers, and legions of fathers, even when they are at home, are a trivial presence—a raw hole in millions of children's lives, and a constant threat to children's moral growth.

What makes matters worse is that these forms of self-interest can proliferate. There is a widespread perception in this country, according to a recent Gallup Poll, not only that the overall state of our morality is "fair or poor," but that it is deteriorating—77 percent of Americans see a decline. And as Joshua Halberstam, a scholar at Teachers College at Columbia University, points out, whether or not this perception is accurate, it can lower our moral expectations and lead us to tolerate unethical behavior.

For example, parents who increasingly perceive each other as vying for an edge for their children can reach a tipping point, so the norm in some communities becomes to advance one's own children with little thought about other people's children. Similarly, fathers who routinely see other fathers taking minimal responsibility for their children can legitimize their neglect of their own kids. And, as Kagan suggests, high-profile scandals like Enron, in which individuals shamelessly pursued their own self-interests, can dangerously reinforce adults' perception that they need to vigilantly protect what's theirs, above other considerations. Many children's tendency to be self-interested is directly affected by this tipping-point phenomenon as well. That cheating has become rampant in American schools is a classic example. There is nothing more devastating to the restraints against cheating than the perception that many others cheat. Almost 60 percent of students in a recent large survey agree with this statement: "In the real world, successful people do what they must to win, even if others consider it cheating."

There is no single cause of these trends. Thoughtful scholars and cultural observers have picked out pieces of the puzzle, including growing wealth among a large sector of the population, which has freed many adults from communal obligations and bonds of reciprocity. To a large extent, the focus on the pursuit of self-interest enshrined in our Declaration of Independence has dangerously mixed in the last forty years with the therapeutic culture. We are living in a time when Americans are more interested not only in their inner states but in their own minute-to-minute well-being than any population in any country in human history —a time, as the cultural critic Philip Rieff put it, when too many people carefully count "satisfactions and dissatisfactions, studying unprofitable commitments as the sins most to be avoided."

And it will take many different kinds of effort to reverse these trends. We need political and cultural leaders who are willing to stand for important principles even at a cost to themselves. We need many more universities that take seriously the character and idealism of their students. We need corporate leaders who are willing to pull back on the pursuit of profits when it collides with basic ethical principles. Yet there are three challenges that are most central, and there are roles for all of us in meeting these challenges.

CHALLENGE NUMBER ONE: EXPECT MORE OF AMERICA'S FATHERS

Our political, religious, and community leaders and many other citizens must develop a more sustained response to obvious forms of moral failure among parents—especially father absence. To focus on evaporating fathers is not, emphatically, to diminish the large numbers of single mothers who are raising strong and caring children. Yet when fathers abandon their children, they are modeling moral irresponsibility, assaulting children's trust, and depriving children of a potentially profound human tie.

At the most basic level, few of these leaders have done anything to stem the tide of father absence. There are important exceptions. Al Gore, as vice president, led an initiative to engage fathers, and organizations such as Promise Keepers and other national groups, as well as scattered local groups, have at various times raised public awareness, worked to connect fathers to children, and struggled to stir in men some sense of moral responsibility.

Yet, in the end, these exceptional efforts have done little to reverse this tide. If women were abandoning children or shirking their responsibilities at this rate, we would see our country as twisted upside down. Nature would seem turned against itself. Concern about father absence tends, on the other hand, to have a flavor-of-the month quality—it has not galvanized a sustained and deep response to a desperate problem.

And the problem is not simply our leaders. Research suggests that fathers who are involved in basic care are more likely to have children who are empathic, generous, and altruistic—and when fathers shirk basic care, it can erode their moral authority—yet little is expected of fathers in their day-to-day interactions with other adults. Fathers are routinely let off the hook for basic care by adults in schools, healthcare institutions, and religious organizations, as well as by employers and colleagues and many other adults who have contact with fathers day to day. Schools, for example, typically don't send report cards to noncustodial fathers or invite them to parent-teacher conferences. Some fathers report that when teachers call their homes—this happened to me on one occasion—the first question they get is: "Is your wife there?" According to research conducted by sociologist James May, healthcare professionals ask fathers one question for every fifteen questions they ask mothers when both are in the room, and rarely make eye contact with fathers.

My point is not to bash teachers or healthcare providers. These professionals are just responding to reality, to the fact that mothers are the primary caretakers of children. I recall reading somewhere about one informal poll showing that about 95 percent of mothers know their children's shoe sizes, in contrast to 5 percent of fathers. My point is that these professionals could be sending quite different messages to fathers, messages that don't let them off the hook for the work of parenting and that communicate basic moral responsibilities. A pediatrician might encourage not just mothers but fathers to attend regular child checkups and make a point of asking fathers not only about their children's well-being but about their relationships with their children. Do their children respect their advice and respond to their attempts to discipline? A minister might ask noncustodial fathers how many times they have seen their child in the last month and ask all fathers in a congregation how many times they have talked to their children in the last month for longer than fifteen minutes. A minister might also ask fathers what they know about their children's capacities for honesty, loyalty, and respect. A school principal might convene a fathers' group that takes as its charge exploring the multiple ways fathers might become more invested in the school community and how fathers can talk to their children about important moral issues. One topic might be how to talk to boys about respecting girls. Employers can clearly make workplaces far more father-friendly, in part because fathers who have strong, healthy families are often more productive. That not only means providing more flexible hours and paternity leave, but modeling engaged fathering and openly crediting those fathers who are active caretakers for their kids.

High-profile symbols and supports for fathers can also encourage them to fulfill their caretaking responsibilities. The fact that baby stations are now in men's restrooms in airports and occasionally in other public places has had both symbolic and practical importance. (A friend recently told me, though, that he was in an airport restroom where a baby station was unfolded and, sure enough, a man in a business suit was standing in front of it. But there wasn't a baby on the table: the man was using the changing table as a desk for his laptop computer.)

CHALLENGE NUMBER TWO: CREATING STRONGER TIES AMONG PARENTS

Reducing parental isolation—giving parents more opportunities to support one another—and creating a sense of communal responsibility for children is a second critical challenge. When parents have trusting, respectful connections with one another, they are more likely both to be effective with their own children and to monitor and guide one another's children. One powerful way to create these ties is to strengthen and expand the growing numbers of family support programs that now dot the country—programs that purposefully try to lace parents together and to cultivate a sense of communal responsibility. "Family support programs create groups for parents based on their common concerns," says Delores Holmes, who directed one of the first family support programs outside Chicago. "And they convey to parents over and over that we are all responsible for each other and that we are much stronger as a unit." Schools, religious organizations, sports programs, childcare centers, and many other community organizations can also do much more to bring families together routinely and to increase parents' sense of responsibility for other people's children.

We as parents can play a vital role in creating these ties as well. In some communities, parents are informally gathering to talk about common problems among teenagers and to develop common responses to predictable teenage troubles. William Damon has advocated for "youth charters"—a shared set of moral expectations and standards for teenagers assembled by parents and a wide array of community leaders and professionals. These kinds of carefully developed mutual understandings are simply not possible in many neighborhoods, given parents' lack of time and disparate views about how to morally steer children. But parents ought to strive for at least some common ground. Parents can agree, for instance, to immediately notify one another if they observe drug use or drinking and driving. Parents can also agree that they will forcefully convey to their children their responsibility for their peers' safety, insisting that their children immediately intervene if a peer is, for instance, sexually bullying or harassing, physically fighting, or abusing drugs.

Parents might also regularly have potlucks and other events that bring families together, especially when there are concerns about neighborhood children. In one neighborhood where I conducted interviews, one family—upset about stigmatizing gossip about a neighborhood teenager who had been arrested twice for stealing clothes from a department store—invited all the families in the neighborhood to a brunch at their house and encouraged other families to host similar events as a way of bringing this boy and his family firmly back into the community. This boy, a very talented trumpet player, played trumpet at this event, enabling neighbors to see him in a positive light.

There are many other ways that we as parents can work to keep marginalized children in the fold. I might have encouraged William to play on other teams I coached, or on teams with other coaches who I thought would connect with him. We might encourage our children to invite marginalized children on certain family outings, or invite them to be part of our religious institutions or observances. I often hear American parents wax nostalgic about an imagined time when communities were close and strong. Yet in these ways we get beyond rhetoric and create the kinds of caring, lasting ties that protect the great many children and families who will be vulnerable at some point in time.

CHALLENGE NUMBER THREE: GIVING EACH OTHER FEEDBACK

How can we create a culture—given our inevitable blind spots as parents—where professionals are more willing to advise and challenge parents, and where parents are more willing to advise and challenge each other? Changing the culture of parenting in this way in this country will clearly not be easy, given that many adults are loath to interfere in other families' private lives. There are also clearly many limits to what kinds of feedback parents can give to each other. My occasional attempts to give feedback to other parents have sometimes succeeded and at other times failed miserably, only making the other parent defensive and angry. I have also received on a few occasions both helpful feedback from other parents and input that seemed way off base and that alienated me. This is a tender, delicate area, and almost any kind of intervention runs the risk of shaming and inflaming parents and making matters worse for a child.

Yet the idea of giving regular feedback, of making parenting more shared, is not novel or radical. In many countries this feedback is routine. In at least some Caribbean countries, for instance, parents expect to receive unsolicited advice from more experienced parents, even parents who are relative strangers.

And when we see a parent acting destructively, we have a responsibility to at least think through how we might constructively influence that parent. We cannot ask children to stand up for their principles or to take actions at a cost to themselves when we as adults protect one another at the expense of children. While deciding whether to intervene should be a difficult balancing act, we need to guard against the strong reflex to avoid the work involved in intervening and the risk of a difficult confrontation.

In most situations where a child is at risk, it is clearly preferable for us to contact a teacher or school counselor or some other trained professional who has the skills and time to engage a family around a problem that is likely to have complex roots. In William's case, looking back to the moment when I first heard from my kids that he wasn't coming to school, I wish I had done some investigating: Did William say whether his parents knew he was skipping school? Did a school counselor or other school adults have William on their radar?

But there are also times when it's not possible or appropriate to engage a professional. We may be concerned, for example, about the destructive parenting practices of a close friend or a sibling or some other relative. I have talked to several parents as they were questioning whether to intervene when a sibling or close friend is indulging his or her child. Yet as siblings or close friends, it may be highly incendiary for us to intervene.

In making these decisions, it may help us to consider several factors. It's important to consider, for example, whether there is any evidence that a child is being harmed, whether our friend or relative respects us, whether this person is too threatened by us in some way to take our feedback to heart, and whether we might have feelings—anger toward this sibling or friend, anxieties or vulnerabilities connected to our own childhood—that are skewing our perspective. If we decide to intervene, our specific approach—the words we choose—will be critical. The chances are much greater that these interventions will be successful if we are speaking as fellow struggling parents, if we convey, along with our concerns, qualities we admire about this parent and his or her child, if we are able to be specific and to provide specific examples, and if we focus on parenting behavior that can be changed, as opposed to ingrained traits that are unlikely to change.

We might create an opening with a parent who is disciplining a child too harshly by saying, "I've always really admired that you're one of those parents who has high expectations for your kid and isn't too permissive. But sometimes I wonder when you ground him so much whether he might just get angry at you and not really learn anything. I'm trying to figure this out with my own kids. What do you think?" We might create an opening for a more extensive conversation with a parent who is indulging a child by saying something like, "You know I really respect you as a parent, but there's one thing I want to mention to you. It seems to me that you may be doing the kind of thing that I find myself doing. I noticed that Jim interrupts you sometimes when you're talking to other people. I don't think I'd let him do that. All of us as parents are trying to make things easy for our kids, but I think we have to remind our kids that we have needs, too. Otherwise, I worry they'll be disrespectful. What do you think?"

Perhaps most important, the effectiveness of these interventions will hinge on whether we have consistently modeled with our intimates a kind of openness—if we have invited these parents to give us feedback and if we have prepared ourselves to respond to that feedback nondefensively. When parents have their first child, they should ask at least one adult they respect, other than a spouse, to promise them that they will provide feedback if they are concerned about a parenting practice that might be harmful. We might also enter into mutual compacts with other parents—at a time when we are not concerned about the others' parenting—mutual assurances of feedback if either parent is acting in any way that might be damaging. These acts, collectively, can begin to change the culture of parenting, creating the norm and expectation that asking for feedback is a basic parental responsibility.

There is a kind of beauty in being a moral person, a beauty that our best novelists and dramatists have evoked since ancient times. We are moved by kindness, generosity, and integrity. We are moved, too, because the deepest forms of morality, of knowing and valuing others, are also the deepest forms of love. And we are awed by the clarity of new moral awareness and by moral transformation—by the capacity of human beings to reckon with their moral failings.

Yet what resonates in our imaginative life we have not taken seriously enough in our actual lives or in our parenting. Too many of us are raising children first and foremost to be happy and we are failing at that project—rather than instilling in them what the novelist William Faulkner thought we as a species needed to prevail: "a spirit capable of compassion and sacrifice and endurance." Too many of us are too aggressive about promoting our children's achievements and too passive about their moral lives. We fail to see something that almost every generation of parents before us has seen clearly—that purposeful, sustained cultivation is needed to promote morality. Too many of us are failing to quarrel with all that is wanting and mistaken in the world around us, let alone asking our children to quarrel with these troubles. And although we know we should reach for our better selves, far too often we don't deal with the obstacles that undermine us as mentors or see in ourselves real moral possibilities. And our failure is expensive to our children.

Yet we are entirely capable of raising children who lead emotionally rich and responsible lives, lives of great integrity and commitment. I am not talking about a life of sanctimony or drudgery or self-righteousness. I am talking about children who as adults experience the necessity—and the wonder and aliveness—of asking moral questions and constructing with others a moral understanding of the world, who listen and reach for moral complexity, search for and follow their higher natures, and engage in vibrant, caring relationships with family and friends. I am talking about children who grow to be alert to signs of distress in other people, who feel responsibility for those from other classes or races or backgrounds, who feel propelled to give to the world in some way. And I am talking about children who develop a sense of obligation to carry forward the highest principles of their ancestors and to protect future generations.

But there is no magic wand. We will have to ask more from our children, we will have to ask more from each other, and we will have to ask more from ourselves.

Introduction

1 *Public Agenda survey, more than six in ten Americans:* Public Agenda, "Americans Deeply Troubled about Nation's Youth; Even Young Children Described by Majority in Negative Terms," press release, June 26, 1997, http://www.publicagenda.org.

6 For a helpful exploration of moral motivation, moral identity, and the moral self, see Gil Noam and Thomas Wren, *The Moral Self* (Cambridge: MIT, 1993). See also Ann Higgins-D'Alessandro and F. Clark Power, "Character, Responsibility, and the Moral Self," in Daniel K. Lapsley and F. Clark Power, eds., *Character Psychology and Character Education* (Notre Dame, IN: University of Notre Dame Press, 2005), 101–20.

5 *Research reveals that even children as young as three and four years old:* Eli H. Newberger, *The Men They Will Become: The Nature and Nurture of Male Character* (Reading, MA: Perseus 1999), 84–85.

7 *Oliner studies:* Cited in James Youniss and Miranda Yates, "Youth Service and Moral-Civic Identity: A Case for Everyday Morality," *Educational Psychology Review* 11, no. 4 (1999): 336; Samuel P. Oliner and Pearl M. Oliner, *The Altruistic Personality: Rescuers of Jews in Nazi Europe* (New York: Free Press, 1988).

1. Helping Children Manage Destructive Emotions

11 *Shame and guilt as the engines of moral learning:* William Damon, *The Moral Child: Nurturing Children's Natural Moral Growth* (New York: Free Press, 1988), 13.
Kagan on violence-prevention programs: Personal communication with Jerome Kagan, 1996.

12 *Almost 75 percent of high school students admit to cheating:* Kevin Ryan, "Character Education: Our High Schools' Missing Link," *Education Week,* published online, January 29, 2003, www.edweek.org (citing a Rutgers University study).
The moral code of gangs rationalizes death as the punishment for disrespect: William Damon makes a similar point in *The Moral Child,* 17–18.

13 *Gilligan quotes on shame and violence:* James Gilligan, "Shame and Humiliation: The Emotions of Individual and Collective Violence"

(paper presented at Erikson Lectures, Harvard University, May 23, 1991).

"Shame of Versailles": James Gilligan, "Shame and Humiliation."

Psychologists viewing shame as a source of narcissism: See, for example, Jan Hoffman, "Here's Looking at Me, Kid," *New York Times*, Sunday Styles, July 20, 2005, 2.

14 *Definition of guilt*: Drawn in part from Robert Karen, "Shame," *Atlantic Monthly*, February 1992, 47.

Karen's observation that shame is about who one is: Karen, "Shame," 47.

Helen Block Lewis quote: in Karen, "Shame," 47.

15 *Marian Wright Edelman's experience*: Marian Wright Edelman, *The Measure of Our Success: A Letter to My Children and Yours* (Boston, Beacon Press, 1992), 3.

Karen on setting children up for shame: Karen, "Shame," 43.

16 *study by psychologist Peggy Miller*: Personal communication with Peggy Miller; and Miller, P. J., Wang, S.-H., Sandel, T. L., Cho, G. E., "Self-esteem as Folk Theory," *Parenting: Science and Practice* 2, no. 3 (2002): 209–39.

John Bradshaw barnstorming the country: Karen, "Shame," 54.

Psychologists claiming that shame is pervasive: A few psychologists I have spoken with make this claim. Robert Karen writes that many psychologists make this claim. Karen, "Shame," 40.

19 *"Nothing is more shameful than to feel ashamed"*: James Gilligan, *Violence: Our Deadly Epidemic and Its Causes* (New York: G. P. Putnam, 1996), 111.

Research showing that affluent families are more likely to keep troubles private: Suniya S. Luthar and Shawn J. Latendresse, "Comparable 'Risks' at the Socioeconomic Status Extremes: Preadolescents' Perceptions of Parenting," *Development and Psychopathology* 17, no. 1 (2005): 224.

Affluent families and the need to maintain a veneer of well-being: J. L. Wolfe and I. G. Fodor, "The Poverty of Privilege: Therapy with Women of the Upper Classes," *Women and Therapy* 18 (1996): 80; cited in Suniya S. Luthar and Shawn J. Latendresse, "Children of the Affluent: Challenges to Well-Being," *Current Directions in Psychological Science* 14, no. 1 (2005): 49.

20 *Middle-class children spending more time with parents during leisure time*: William Damon, *Greater Expectations: Overcoming the Culture*

of Indulgence in America's Homes and Schools (New York: Free Press, 1995), 28.

First Lewis quote: In Karen, "Shame," 61.

Second Lewis quote: Michael Lewis, *Shame: The Exposed Self* (New York: Free Press, 1992), 111. This paragraph is also based on a conversation with Michael Lewis, 2006.

21 *Children may find themselves feeling hostile toward their parents, and wind up ashamed of these feelings as well*: Karen makes a similar point. Karen, "Shame," 64.

22 For wisdom about and strategies for punishing effectively, see Kazdin, Alan E., *The Kazdin Method for Parenting the Defiant Child* (Boston: Houghton Mifflin, 2008).

24 *Depressed parents fastening on their children's flaws and study indicating that the longer fathers are unemployed, the more likely they are to describe their children negatively*: Vonnie C. McLoyd, "The Impact of Economic Hardship on Black Families and Children," *Child Development* 61, no. 2 (1990): 328.

Beardslee on the importance of self-awareness: William Beardslee, *When a Parent Is Depressed: How to Protect Your Children from Depression in the Family* (Boston: Little, Brown, 2003), and personal communication with William Beardslee, 2005.

26 *Peer groups' positive influences*: Ritch C. Savin-Williams and Thomas J. Berndt, "Friendship and Peer Relations," in S. Shirley Feldman and Glen R. Elliot, eds., *At the Threshold: The Developing Adolescent* (Cambridge, MA: Harvard University Press, 1990), 297.

27 *Children more likely to think and act independently if they have parents who respect their capacity to think*: This finding is suggested by the research of Samuel P. Oliner and Pearl M. Oliner, *The Altruistic Personality: Rescuers of Jews in Nazi Europe* (New York: Free Press, 1988), 171–86.

Children more likely to withstand peer disapproval if they have input into family decisions: This connection is suggested by research indicating that children who have input into family decisions are more likely to have positive self-esteem, one form of protection against peer disapproval. Jacqueline S. Eccles et al., "Development during Adolescence: The Impact of Stage-Environment Fit in Young Adolescents' Experiences in Schools and in Families," *American Psychologist* 48, no. 2 (1993): 98.

Girls' capacity for self-assertion as going "underground": Lyn Mikel

Brown and Carol Gilligan, *Meeting at the Crossroads: Women's Psychology and Girls' Development* (Cambridge, MA: Harvard University Press, 1992).

29 *The interpersonal nature of the self in adolescence*: Robert Kegan, *The Evolving Self: Problem and Process in Human Development* (Cambridge, MA: Harvard University Press, 1982); see, especially, 57. Notes from Robert Kegan lecture, Harvard Graduate School of Education, 1982.

30 *Severe punishments distract children from moral messages*: Damon, *Greater Expectations*, 179–81.

Time *magazine article on adolescence*: Melissa Ludtke, "Through the Eyes of Children," *Time*, August 8, 1988, 55.

T*he book* A Tribe Apart: Patricia Hersch, *A Tribe Apart: A Journey into the Heart of American Adolescence* (New York: Ballantine, 1999).

31 *Research on adolescent self-representations*: Daniel Hart and Suzanne Fegley, "Prosocial Behavior and Caring in Adolescence: Relations to Self-Understanding and Social Judgment," *Child Development* 66 (1995): 1347.

Anna Freud on adolescent rebellion: Anna Freud, *The Ego and the Mechanisms of Defense* (1937), cited in Robert Coles, *The Moral Life of Children* (Boston: Atlantic Monthly Press, 1986), 164.

34 *What it means to believe in yourself*: William Damon, *Greater Expectations*, 81.

2. *Promoting Happiness and Morality*

38 For a valuable discussion of the social and emotional skills needed to treat people well, see Amelie Rorty, "What It Takes to Be Good," in eds. Gil G. Noam and Thomas E. Wren, *The Moral Self* (Cambridge, MA: MIT Press, 1993), 28–55.

Infants are visibly upset when they hear other infants crying: Daniel Goleman, *Emotional Intelligence* (New York: Bantam Books, 1995), 98.

Daniel Stern on "attunement": Goleman, *Emotional Intelligence*, 100.

40 *Focus on children's happiness in the 1920s and 1930s*: Steven Mintz, *Huck's Raft: A History of American Childhood* (Cambridge, MA: The Belknap Press of Harvard University Press, 2004); see especially p. 219. Also, personal communication with Steven Mintz, 2008.

42 *Contrast in college students' goals between 1970 and 2005*: Census Bureau finding cited in Jim Holt, "You Are What You Expect," *New York Times Magazine*, January 21, 2007.

43 *Epicurus on happiness*: Mihaly Csikszentmihalyi, "If We Are So Rich,

Why Aren't We Happy?" *American Psychologist* 54 (October 1999): 821–22.

College students in the past who disdained happiness as shallow: Maureen Dowd makes this point as well. Maureen Dowd, "Happiness Is a Warm Gun," *New York Times,* March 25, 2006.

Commentary pages *and* Doonesbury *panels lampooning the self-esteem movement:* Alfie Kohn, "The Truth About Self-Esteem," *Phi Delta Kappan* 76 (December 1994): 272; Chester E. Finn Jr., "Narcissus Goes to School," *Commentary,* June 1990, 40.

46 *Research showing that gang leaders, violent criminals, delinquents, and bullies can have high self-esteem:* Roy Baumeister, Laura Smart, and Joseph Boden, "Relation of Threatened Egotism to Violence and Aggression: The Dark Side of High Self-Esteem," *Psychological Review* 103, no. 1 (1996); and Elizabeth Svoboda, "Everyone Loves a Bully," *Psychology Today,* March–April 2004, 20, citing a study by University of California-Los Angeles psychologist Jaana Juvonen.

John Stuart Mill quote: Alex Beam, "The Secret to Happiness? Who Knows?" *Boston Globe,* May 20, 2008.

47 *Darrin McMahon quote on forsaking nobility:* Harvey Mansfield, review of Darrin M McMahon's *Happiness: A History* (New York: Atlantic Monthly Press, 2006), in *New Republic,* July 3, 2006, 32.

Book promoting the idea that being a good person is the key to health and a longer life: Stephen Post and Jill Neimark, *Why Good Things Happen to Good People: The Exciting New Research That Proves the Link Between Doing Good and Living a Longer, Healthier, Happier Life* (New York: Broadway Books, 2007).

48 *Dimpies—doting indulgent modern parents:* Scot Lehigh, "Parents, Behave!" *Boston Globe,* March 28, 2006.

49 *Modern parents' investment in entertaining their children:* William Damon, *Greater Expectations: Overcoming the Culture of Indulgence in America's Homes and Schools* (New York: Free Press, 1995), 109–110.

51 *Children thrive on praise when it is specific:* Po Bronson, "How Not to Talk to Your Kids," *New York Magazine,* February 12, 2007, 5, citing Carol Dweck's research, Stanford University.

Sports program recommending 5:1 ratio of praise to criticism: Positive Coaching Alliance, http://www.positivecoach.org, 2007.

52 *Children and empty flattery:* Damon, *Greater Expectations,* 74.

Wulf-Uwe Meyer on how children view praise: Cited in Po Bronson, "How Not to Talk to Your Kids," 6.

Research on deleterious behavior of children who are praised too much: Po Bronson, "How Not to Talk to Your Kids," 6, again citing Carol Dweck's research, Stanford University.

Dangers of global praise: Robert Karen, "Shame," *Atlantic Monthly*, February 1992, 62.

55 *"Time is how you spend your love"*: Zadie Smith, *On Beauty: A Novel* (New York: Penguin Press, 2005), acknowledgments.

60 *The sense of self becoming significant in the nineteenth century*: Damon, *Greater Expectations*, 68.

3. The Real Danger in the Achievement Craze

62 *The "brain time" slogan and a third of American children have seen a Baby Einstein video*: Alissa Quart, "Extreme Parenting: Does the Baby Genius Edutainment Complex Enrich Your Child's Mind—or Stifle It?" *Atlantic Monthly*, July/August 2006.

Parents procuring tutors for preschool children: Marek Fuchs, "Tutoring Gives Pupils an Edge . . . for Preschool," *New York Times*, July 31, 2002.

"Millions of families are now in a state of nervous collapse" and kids fearing their life will be "ruined": Gregg Easterbrook, "Who Needs Harvard?" *Atlantic Monthly*, October 2004, 128.

63 *The pressure to do well being up and the demand to be good being down*: Judith Warner, "Kids Gone Wild," *New York Times*, November 27, 2005.

"My kid sells term papers to your honors student": Stephanie Rosenbloom, "Honk If You Adore My Child Too," *New York Times*, January 5, 2006.

65 *High rates of behavior problems and delinquency in affluent communities*: Suniya S. Luthar and Shawn J. Latendresse, "Children of the Affluent: Challenges to Well-Being," *Current Directions in Psychological Science* 14, no. 1 (2005): 3.

Affluent children experiencing higher levels of drug use (including hard drugs), anxiety, and depression, and suburban girls being three times more likely to be depressed: Suniya S. Luthar and Bronwyn E. Becker, "Privileged but Pressured?: A Study of Affluent Youth," *Child Development* 73, no. 5 (2002): 1593.

Link between children's troubles and achievement pressures and risks for children with perfectionist strivings: Luthar and Becker, "Privileged but Pressured?" 1605; and Luthar and Latendresse, "Children of the Affluent," 2.

68 *Alice Miller on children closeting their feelings:* Alice Miller, *The Drama of the Gifted Child* (New York: Basic Books, 1981).
What Luthar and Latendresse call a "meager sense of self": Luthar and Latendresse, "Children of the Affluent," 4.

70 *Ariel Karlin on her mother's anecdotes about "psycho moms":* Ariel Karlin, "The Parent Paradox," *U.S. News & World Report,* America's Best Colleges, August 29, 2005, 23.

71 *Ariel Karlin on Peruvian farming:* Karlin, "The Parent Paradox," 23.

73 *Arlie Hochschild on parents' passing on their status via their kids' skills:* In Stephanie Rosenbloom, "Honk If You Adore My Child Too," *New York Times,* January 5, 2006.

74 *Children subjected to intense pressure to achieve don't outperform other students:* Luthar and Becker, "Privileged but Pressured?" 1603.
Too much focus on high achievement makes adults fragile, vulnerable: Suniya Luthar and Shawn J. Latendresse, "Comparable 'Risks' at the Socioeconomic Extremes: Preadolescents' Perceptions of Parenting," *Development and Psychopathology* 17, no. 1 (2005): 208–9.
Juvenile delinquency spiking when neglectful parenting is combined with achievement pressure: This was suggested by my conversations with school staff. See also Luthar and Becker, "Privileged but Pressured?" 1603.
On parents rationalizing or taking pride in children's college choices: Andrew Hacker makes a similar point in "The Truth about Colleges," *New York Review of Books,* November 3, 2005, 51.

77 *Alissa Quart on parents fearing their children will be ordinary:* Alissa Quart, *Hothouse Kids: The Dilemma of the Gifted Child* (New York: Penguin Press, 2006), quoted in Tsing Loh, "The Drama of the Gifted Parent," 116.

78 *Wendy Mogel on the twenty-minute rule:* In Emily Bazelon, "So the Torah Is a Parenting Guide?" *New York Times Magazine,* October 1, 2006, 67.

79 *Sandra Tsing Loh on college students' rebelling by burning* U.S. News & World Report *college rankings:* Tsing Loh, "The Drama of the Gifted Parent," 118.

4. When Being Close to Children Backfires

81 *Statistics on fathers providing care for their children:* Julia Overturf Johnson, "Who's Minding the Kids? Child Care Arrangements: Winter 2002," *Household Economic Studies, Current Population Reports,* U.S. Census Bureau (October 2005); 19.

82 *Statistics on children losing contact with their fathers*: Judith A. Seltzer, "Child Support and Child Access: Experiences of Divorced and Non-marital Families," in *Child Support: The Next Frontier*, ed. J. Thomas Oldman and Marygold S. Melli (Ann Arbor: University of Michigan Press, 2000), 73.

85 *The development of identity in adolescence*: See Erik H. Erikson, *Identity, Youth, and Crisis* (New York: Norton, 1968). See especially p. 87.
Adults have organizing narrative: Susan Harter et al., "The Development of Multiple Role-Related Selves during Adolescence," *Development and Psychopathology* 9 (December 1997): 850.

86 *Donna Wick on parents relinquishing gratifying self-images*: Personal communication with Donna Wick, 2006.

88 *The Mother-Daughter Project*: See SuEllen Hamkins and Renée Schultz, *The Mother-Daughter Project: How Mothers and Daughters Can Band Together, Beat the Odds, and Thrive through Adolescence* (New York: Hudson Street Press, 2007).
Wick on mom who struggles with her infant's separations: Donna Wick, "Reflective-Functioning and Self-Awareness: A Longitudinal Study of Attachment and Caregiving Representations in Three Mothers" (doctoral thesis, Graduate School of Education, Harvard University, 2004), see especially pp. 77, 99, 106.
Web cameras at camp: Judith Warner, "Loosen the Apron Strings," *New York Times*, July 20, 2006.
Sneaking cell phones and badgering camp staff: See Tina Kelley, "Dear Parents: Please Relax, It's Just Camp," *New York Times*, July 26, 2008.
Students planning to move home post-college: Monster Job Survey.
Percent of eighteen- to twenty-five-year-olds who say they have talked to their parents in the past day: Ann Hulbert, "Beyond the Pleasure Principle," *New York Times Magazine*, March 11, 2007, 15. Citing the Pew Research Center for the People & the Press, *A Portrait of "Next Generation": How Young People View Their Lives, Futures and Politics* (Washington, DC: Pew Research Center for the People & the Press, January 9, 2007).

89 *Kagan on how the parenting of young children can create fragility*: In Hara E. Marano, "A Nation of Wimps," *Psychology Today*, November–December 2004, 7.
College staff worrying that parents are far too involved with young people: See, for example, Bridget Booher, "Helicopter Parents," *Duke Magazine*, January–February 2007, 26.

"I wish my parents had some hobby other than me": Quoted in Marano, "A Nation of Wimps," 5.

"Teacups" and "krispies": Emily Bazelon, "So the Torah Is a Parenting Guide?" *New York Times Magazine*, October 1, 2006, p. 64, quoting clinical psychologist Wendy Mogel.

90 *Research pointing to the value of regular family dinners*: Suniya Luthar and Shawn J. Latendresse, "Children of the Affluent: Challenges to Well-Being," *Current Directions in Psychological Science* 14, no. 1 (2005): 3.

91 *The self develops through mirroring and idealization of parents*: Heinz Kohut, *The Restoration of the Self* (New York: International Universities Press, 1977). For a useful summary, see P. J. Watson, Tracy Little, and Michael D. Biderman, "Narcissism and Parenting Styles," *Journal of Psychoanalytic Psychology* 9, no. 2 (1992): 232.

92 *Kohut on "optimal frustration"*: Kohut, *The Restoration of the Self*, as summarized in Watson, Little, and Biderman, "Narcissism and Parenting Styles," 232.

94 *"We are trying to show the kids how much we trust them"*: Melissa Ludtke, "Through the Eyes of Children," *Time*, August 8, 1988, 57.

96 *Parents have fewer confidants*: This is based on a General Social Survey finding that American adults have markedly fewer confidants in 2004 than they did in 1985. Anne Hulbert, "Confidant Crisis," *New York Times Magazine*, July 16, 2006.

5. Moral Adults: Moral Children

99 *Brothers Grimm fairy tale "The Old Grandfather and the Grandson"*: *Fairy Tales by the Grimm Brothers*, Authorama: Public Domain Books, http://www.authorama.com/grimms-fairy-tales-27.html.

100 *Percentage of adults belonging to self-help or support groups*: Robert Wuthnow, *Sharing the Journey: Support Groups and America's New Quest for Community* (New York: Free Press, 1994), 71. David Grand, *Emotional Healing at Warp Speed: The Power of EMDR* (New York: Harmony Books, 2001).

On some adults not developing serious ideals until midlife: See, for example, Anne Colby and William Damon, *Some Do Care: Contemporary Lives of Moral Commitment* (New York: Free Press, 1992).

Research showing that the elderly become more other-centered: Kevin Cool, "New Age Thinking," *Stanford Magazine* (Stanford Alumni Association), July–August 2004, 54, citing the findings of Stanford University researcher Laura Carstensen.

101 *The development in later adulthood of moral strengths including em-*
pathy: For a related discussion see Louis Menand, "Name That Tone,"
New Yorker, June 26, 2006.
Gil Noam on moral maturity in adult life: Gil G. Noam, "Reconceptu-
alizing Maturity: The Search for Deeper Meaning," in *Development*
and Vulnerability in Close Relationships, ed. Gil G. Noam and Kurt
W. Fischer (Mahwah, NJ: Lawrence Erlbaum, 1996).
Depressed mothers and low-birth-weight babies: S. Parker et al., "Dou-
ble Jeopardy: The Impact of Poverty on Early Child Development,"
Pediatric Clinics of North America 35, no. 6 (1988): 3.

102 *"There is nothing noble in being superior to someone else . . .":* The
quote is a Hindu proverb that has been attributed to Young, among
others.

105 *These stages of parents' perspective-taking are drawn in part from Rob-*
ert Selman's work on perspective-taking: Selman, a psychologist at
Harvard University, describes several stages of perspective-taking—
children can develop from understanding their own perspectives, to
understanding others' perspectives, to coordinating their own perspective and another person's perspective, to coordinating multiple perspectives and a generalized, third-person perspective. At the
highest stage children can come to see how a relationship functions
within the context of both their own history and life and within the
context of another person's history and life: Robert L. Selman, *The*
Growth of Interpersonal Understanding: Developmental and Clinical
Analyses (New York: Academic Press, 1980). While Selman has focused on children, the development of these perspective-taking capacities can continue throughout adult life. Here I'm applying Selman's framework to shed light on parents' capacities to take the
perspective of older children primarily. I'm indebted, too, to Donna
Wick's dissertation, "Reflective-Functioning and Self-Awareness: A
Longitudinal Study of Attachment and Caregiving Representations
in Three Mothers" (Graduate School of Education, Harvard University, 2004), where she summarizes and draws on Selman's work to
analyze the perspective-taking capacities of parents of young children.

106 *Percentage of parents suffering a major depression:* William R. Beardslee, *When a Parent Is Depressed* (Boston: Little, Brown, 2003).
Children of depressed parents are more likely to abuse drugs and to be-
come depressed themselves: Jane Brody, "Personal Health; Depressed

Parent's Children At Risk," *New York Times*, March 3, 1998, citing the work of Myrna M. Weissman at Yale University.
Children of depressed parents more likely to suffer behavior problems: H. Orvaschel, G. Welsh-Allis, and W. Ye, "Psychopathology in Children of Parents with Recurrent Depression," *Journal of Abnormal Child Psychology* 16 (1988): 17–28. See especially p. 21.

107 *Fraiberg on "ghosts in the nursery"*: Selma Fraiberg, Edna Adelsen, and Vivian Shapiro, "Ghosts in the Nursery: A Psychoanalytic Approach to the Problems of Impaired Infant-Mother Relationships," in *Selected Writings of Selma Fraiberg*, ed. Louis Fraiberg (Columbus: Ohio State University Press, 1987), 100.

109 *Mother hitting her children "because they were the only things . . . I could control"*: Quoted in Felicia R. Lee, "Where Parents Are Learning to Be Parents," *New York Times*, March 14, 1993.
Beardslee on parents being ashamed to talk about depression, and how that effects children: Personal communication with Beardslee, 2000.
Donna Wick on mother with separation difficulties: D. Wick, "Reflective-Functioning and Self-Awareness," see especially p. 65.

112 *Great strides in treating depression — 80 percent of people are helped*: This figure was cited by William Beardslee in a talk he gave in Cambridge, Mass., in 2007. In a personal communication following the talk, Beardslee explained that in many randomized trials where the treatment group either receives cognitive therapy or medication, the usual response rate is about 70 percent, compared to somewhere between 30 and 40 percent in the placebo group. If a second treatment is added, either a change in medication or a change in modalities, usually the rate of helpful treatment goes up by 10 percent.
Severity or duration of parents' destructive moods often less damaging than how children understand them: William Beardslee, *When a Parent Is Depressed*, and personal communication with Beardslee, 2008.

114 *Wick describes how in the literature infants grow but mothers don't change:* D. Wick, "Reflective-Functioning and Self-Awareness," p. 17.
"Like gray hair and attenuated muscles": Harvard V. Knowles and David Weber, "The Residential School as a Moral Environment," in *Knowledge without Goodness Is Dangerous: Moral Education in Boarding Schools*, ed. Charles L. Terry (Exeter, NH: Phillips Exeter Academy Press, 1981), 87.

6. The Real Moral Power of Schools

116   *American schools conceived to build character:* Michael B. Katz, *Improving Poor People: The Welfare State, the "Underclass," and Urban Schools as History* (Princeton, NJ: Princeton University Press, 1995), especially 103–5. James D. Hunter, *The Death of Character: Moral Education in an Age without Good or Evil* (New York: Basic Books, 2000), chapter 3.

Polls showing that Americans want schools to teach standards of right and wrong and values: Hunter, *The Death of Character.*

Research suggesting that parents doubt their capacities as moral mentors: Alan Wolfe, *Moral Freedom: The Search for Virtue in a World of Choice* (New York: W. W. Norton, 2001).

A billion-dollar values industry: J. D. Hunter, *The Death of Character,* 4.

118   *Adults manipulating the rhetoric of morality:* Harvard V. Knowles and David Weber, "The Residential School as a Moral Environment," in *Knowledge without Goodness Is Dangerous: Moral Education in Boarding Schools,* ed. Charles L. Terry (Exeter, NH: Phillips Exeter Academy Press, 1981), 87.

The full, powerful quote is:

> What we urge more positively is chiefly a set of perspectives: there is nothing inherently noble in adulthood; there is nothing inherently evil or embarrassing in adolescence. If we see that our students are amorphous, confused or contradictory, that they sometimes act badly, we should not be deceived into thinking they are different in kind from ourselves. That they are in a different stage of development does not make them inferior or less human. Indeed, perhaps we should begin to see that their apparent moral amorphousness is more like our own condition than we are willing to admit. Maybe we are not so much more certain about our moral beliefs as we are more adept at manipulating the rhetoric of morality. If this is indeed the case, perhaps a truly moral educational environment is one that is open to question, that is responsive to the evolving ethical codes of the community, that is secure enough in terms of its own first principals to entertain questions about values and attitudes. What kind of moral statement does our educational environment make when it implies through the attitude of its teachers

*that values become fixed with age, that moral behavior, like gray
hair and attenuated muscles, comes inevitably with the passage
of time? Students should see that a moral position comes from
struggle, that it is often expensively wrung from awesomely
complex patterns of pain and injustice. To present them a
community smug in its assertion of right and wrong, unyielding
in its insistence on imposing its values on others, is to present
them a model inconsistent with the experience of reflective
people. We need to see ourselves not just as teachers but as
people; we need to accept our own humanness, our own frailty,
our own capacity for growth, as a precondition for accepting our
students.*

119 *John Dewey on politeness and formalism:* Sara Lawrence-Lightfoot, *The Essential Conversation: What Parents and Teachers Can Learn from Each Other* (New York: Random House, 2003), 79. This powerful, wise book was generally helpful in shaping the ideas of this chapter.

120 *Low-income parents not feeling entitled to advocate:* A terrific organization, The Right Question Project in Cambridge, MA, was started to strengthen low-income parents' capacity to advocate effectively for their children in schools.

121 *Thompson on parentectomy:* Michael Thompson, "The Fear Equation," *Independent School* 55, no. 3 (Spring 1996): 52.
Thompson on "the Volvo caucus": Thompson, "The Fear Equation," 47.
Teachers being judged by biased parents: Lawrence-Lightfoot, *The Essential Conversation,* 78.

123 *Ghosts in classroom:* Lawrence-Lightfoot, *The Essential Conversation,* 3.

125 *Teachers fear that administrators can't protect them:* Thompson, "The Fear Equation," 52.

127 *Using "we" in parent-teacher conferences:* Lawrence-Lightfoot, *The Essential Conversation,* 169.

128 *Students still focus on the strengths and weaknesses of individual teachers after school reform:* Judith W. Little, Rena Dorph, et al., *California's School Restructuring Demonstration Program* (Berkeley: University of California, 1998), 44, 49.

130 *Mary Burchenal poem "The Parent Conference":* Mary Burchenal is a teacher at Brookline High School, Brookline, Massachusetts.

One-half of new teachers nationally leave profession within five years: For data on teachers leaving the profession, see Richard M. Ingersoll, "The Teacher Shortage: A Case of Wrong Diagnosis and Wrong Prescription," *NASSP Bulletin* 86, no. 631 (2002): 16–30; National Commission on Teaching and America's Future, *No Dream Denied: A Pledge to America's Children* (New York: National Commission on Teaching and America's Future, 2003); E. Fidler and D. Haselkorn, *Learning the Roles: Urban Teacher Induction Practices in the United States* (Belmont, MA: Recruiting New Teachers, 1999).

132 *Teachers' mapping relationships with students in Anchorage, Alaska:* Nancy Walser, "'R' is for Resilience," *Harvard Education Letter* 22, no. 5 (September–October 2006): 1–3.

134 *Children more likely to embrace a value when they arrive at it through their own thinking:* Alfie Kohn, quoting John Holt, makes a similar point in "How Not to Teach Values: A Critical Look at Character Education," *Phi Beta Kappan* 78, no. 6 (February 1997): 429–39.
Thomas Lickona quote: Personal communication with Thomas Lickona, 2008.

7. The Morally Mature Sports Parent

137 *Report by the National Alliance for Youth Sports:* National Alliance for Youth Sports, *Recommendations for Communities,* developed through the National Summit on Raising Community Standards in Children's Sports (West Palm Beach, FL: National Alliance for Youth Sports, January 2002), 13, http://www.nays.org/IntMain.cfm?Page=120&Cat=20#1.
More than 40 million American children engaged in sports: David E. Williams, "Character Builder or Pressure-Cooker: Parents and Youth Sports," CNN.com, July 10, 2006, citing data from the National Council of Youth Sports.
Sports keeping kids out of harm's way: Research indicates that sports participation is, in fact, negatively correlated with delinquency and may prevent gang involvement. See Vern Seefeldt and Martha Ewing, "Youth Sports in America: An Overview," *PCPFS Research Digest*, series 2, no. 11 (1996).

138 *Decisions in sports as having parallels in other areas of life:* See David Shields and Brenda J. Bredemeier, *Character Development and Physical Activity* (Champaign, IL: Human Kinetics, 1994), cited in Jeffrey Pratt Beedy and Tom Zierk, "Lessons from the Field: Taking a Proac-

tive Approach to Developing Character Through Sports," *CYD Journal* 1, no. 3 (2000): 1.

Gillespie on sports as offering a "concrete experience of justice": Michael A. Gillespie, "Players and Spectators: Sports and Ethical Training in the American University," in *Morality and Education*, ed. Elizabeth Kiss and Peter Euben, forthcoming.

Gillespie on pickup sports: Gillespie, "Players and Spectators: Sports and Ethical Training in the American University."

141 *Geertz on sports as "deep play"*: Clifford Geertz, "Deep Play: Notes on the Balinese Cockfight," *Daedalus* 134 (Winter 1972): 2, quoted in Gillespie, "Players and Spectators."

Meaning of sports for the ancient Greeks and the British: See, for example, Gillespie, "Players and Spectators: Sports and Ethical Training in the American University."

Heywood Hale Broun on sports revealing character: Cited in Beedy and Zierk, "Lessons from the Field," 1.

142 *Children playing "tug of peace"*: Brian O'Conner, "Shaughnessey's Senior Year Touches All the Bases," Review of Dan Shaughnessey, *Senior Year: A Father, A Son, and High School Baseball, Boston Globe,* Book Review section, May 27, 2007.

143 *Functioning in sports does not predict functioning in life*: This finding is suggested by J. W. McFarlane, "Perspectives on Personality Consistency and Change from the Guidance Study," *Vita Humana* 7 (1964): 115–26.

147 *Research suggesting that some children continue to play sports to please their parents*: J. C. Hellstedt, "Early Adolescent Perceptions of Parental Pressure in the Sport Environment," *Journal of Sport Behavior* 13 (1990): 135–144. Cited in eds. R. Hedstrom and D. Gould, "Research in Youth Sports: Critical Issues Status," Institute for the Study of Youth Sports, College of Education, Michigan State University, East Lansing, MI (11/01/04): 29.

148 Friday Night Lights *quote*: H. G. Bissinger, *Friday Night Lights: A Town, a Team, and a Dream* (Da Capo Press, 1990), 20.

149 *"Like most men, I'd wanted a son who reminded me of myself . . ."*: Tom Perrotta, "The Smile on Happy Chang's Face," *Post Road Magazine* 8 (2003), reprinted in *The Best American Short Stories*, ed. Michael Chabon (Boston: Houghton Mifflin, 2005), 9.

150 *Narrator in Perrotta's short story wants one team to "humiliate" the other*: Perrotta, "The Smile on Happy Chang's Face," 1.

The sports consultant Greg Dale's recommendations to parents: Dale's ideas and quotes in this chapter are taken from a talk he gave in Cambridge, Massachusetts, in 2006, and from his book, *The Fulfilling Ride: A Parent's Guide to Helping Athletes Have a Successful Sport Experience* (Durham, NC: Excellence in Performance, 2005).

153 *Documentary film* The Heart of the Game: *The Heart of the Game*, written and directed by Ward Serrell (Woody Creek Productions and Miramax Films in association with Flying Spot Pictures, 2005).

155 *Parental entitlement being less of a norm in working-class communities*: See, for example, Annette Lareau, *Unequal Childhoods: Class, Race, and Family Life* (Berkeley: University of California Press, 2003).

156 *The sports consultants Jeff Beedy and Tom Zierk recommend*: The quotes and suggestions from Jeff Beedy and Tom Zierk throughout this chapter are from personal communication with Beedy and Zierk.

158 *Quote from* Remember the Titans, *"This is no democracy"*: Cited in David Brooks, "Remaking the Epic of America," *New York Times,* Week in Review, February 5, 2006.
Sports coaches in films who stand for racial and social justice: David Brooks, "Remaking the Epic of America."
70 percent of kids quit sports by age thirteen: Eli Newberger, *The Men They Will Become: The Nature and Nurture of Male Character* (Reading, MA: Perseus, 1999), 308, citing data from the National Alliance for Youth Sports.

163 *Massachusetts sports contract for parents*: "Sport Parent Code of Conduct," Document developed by the Massachusetts Governor's Committee on Physical Fitness and Sports and the National Youth Sports Safety Foundation on Sept. 23, 2000: http://www.nyssf.org/sportparentcodeofconduct.html.

8. Cultivating Mature Idealism in Young People

166 *Templeton Foundation on colleges that are serious about moral development*: John Templeton Foundation, http://www.templeton.org.
Harry Lewis quotation: Harry R. Lewis, *Excellence Without a Soul: How a Great University Forgot Education* (New York: Public Affairs, 2006), quoted in Andrew Delbanco, "Scandals of Higher Education," *New York Review of Books,* March 29, 2007.
David Brooks's observation on universities: David Brooks, "The Organization Kid," *Atlantic Monthly,* April 2001, 53.

167 *Young adults appointing older adults as "guardians of a final identity":* Erik Erikson, *Childhood and Society* (New York: Norton, 1963), 261.

169 *Newberger quote on impure motives and idealism:* Eli H. Newberger, *The Men They Will Become: The Nature and Nurture of Male Character* (Reading, MA: Perseus, 1999), 322.

172 *Connection of young people's voting to their parents' civic engagement:* Alissa Quart, "They're Not Buying It," *New York Times,* November 6, 2004.

173 *Brooks on conformity of young people:* David Brooks, "The Organization Kid," 41, cited in Scott Seider, *Literature, Justice and Resistance: Engaging Adolescents from Privileged Groups in Social Action* (doctoral thesis, Harvard Graduate School of Education, 2008). See p. 17 of this thesis for more information about young people's conformity. This superb dissertation also generally illuminates the pathways and obstacles to developing ideals.

9. Key Moral Strengths of Children Across Race and Culture

179 *One in five American children now live in an immigrant family:* Ron Haskins, Mark Greenberg, and Shawn Fremstad, "Federal Policy for Immigrant Children: Room for Common Ground," policy brief that is a companion piece to *Future of Children* 14, no. 2 (2004): 1.

Rise in percentage of children living in immigrant families: Michael Fix and Jeffrey S. Passel, *U.S. Immigration: Trends and Implications for Schools* (Washington, DC: Urban Institute January 28, 2003), http://www.urban.org/url.cfm?ID=410654.

First-generation immigrant children faring better on these measures than American-born counterparts: See, for example, Donald J. Hernandez and Evan Charney, eds., *From Generation to Generation: The Health and Well-Being of Children in Immigrant Families* (Washington, DC: National Academy Press, 1998), 6; Laurence Steinberg, with B. Bradford Brown and Sanford M. Dornbusch, *Beyond the Classroom: Why School Reform Has Failed and What Parents Need to Do* (New York: Simon & Schuster, 1996), 98.

Importance of the kind of communities immigrant children land in: Min Zhou, "Growing Up American: The Challenge Confronting Immigrant Children and Children of Immigrants," *Annual Review of Sociology* 23 (1997): 66.

Inverse relationship between English proficiency and school performance: Carola Suárez-Orozco and Marcelo M. Suárez-Orozco, *Children of Immigration* (Cambridge, MA: Harvard University Press,

2001), 5, citing research of sociologists Ruben Rumbaut and Ale-
jandro Portes.

*Increases in substance abuse and delinquency the longer immigrant
children are here:* See, for example, Hernandez and Charney, *From
Generation to Generation,* 6.

Marcelo Suárez-Orozco quote: Personal communication, 2001.

180   *Third-generation immigrant children faring as bad or worse on most
mental health or moral measures:* See, for example, Hernandez and
Charney, *From Generation to Generation,* 6; Steinberg, *Beyond the
Classroom,* 97–98.

*Mexico sends the most children, followed by the Philippines, China,
and India:* Migration Policy Institute, Washington, DC, 2008.

*Immigrant parents more comfortable asserting authority, demanding
respect, holding their children to high standards:* A. J. Fuligni, V. Tseng,
and M. Lam, "Attitudes Toward Family Obligations among American Adolescents with Asian, Latin American and European Backgrounds," *Child Development* 70, no. 4 (1999): 1030–31.

*New research revealing that many Asian and Latino parents are fo-
cused on certain forms of individualism in their children:* C. S. Tamis-
LeMonda et al., "Parents' Goals for Children: The Dynamic Co-
Existence of Collectivism and Individualism in Cultures and
Individuals," *Social Development* 17, no. 1 (2008): 183–209.

Many immigrant families highly focused on individual achievement:
See, for example, Fuligni, Tseng, and Lam, "Attitudes Toward Family
Obligations," 1031.

181   *Research suggesting that Asian American and Latin American children are more likely than their peers to attend to family needs, etc.:*
Fuligni, Tseng, and Lam, "Attitudes Toward Family Obligations,"
1030–1031.

*David Brooks on immigrant families as antidote to excessive individu-
alism:* David Brooks, "Immigrants to Be Proud Of," *New York Times,*
March 30, 2006.

182   *Negative peer influences on immigrant kids:* See, for example, Steinberg, *Beyond the Classroom,* 98–99.

183   *Research indicating parent-child fractures in a wide range of immigrant
families:* See, for example, Zhou, "Growing Up American," 84–85.

184   *Immigrant parents worrying that their children are becoming selfish:*
Tamis-LeMonda et al., "Parents' Goals for Children."

Immigrant children sometimes being embarrassed by parents: Zhou,
"Growing Up American," 84.

Mary Waters's quotes on immigrant children and their parents' jobs: Personal communication with Mary Waters, 2001.

185 *The high-wire act of immigrant parents in developing children's "bicultural competencies"*: Suárez-Orozco and Suárez-Orozco, *Children of Immigration*, 7.

187 *Mary Casey's findings in a southern high school*: See Mary Casey, "Living with Difference: Race and the Development of Critical Perspectives on Goodness" (Cambridge, MA: Harvard Graduate School of Education), unpublished paper, 2002, 18–20. Also personal communication with Mary Casey, 2007.

Wiseman's documentary film: High School II, written, directed, and produced by Frederick Wiseman (Zipporah Films Productions, 1994).

188 *Janie Ward and W. E. B. Du Bois and dual reality*: Carol Gilligan and Janie Ward, foreword to Vanessa S. Walker and John R. Snarey, eds., *Race-ing Moral Formation: African-American Perspectives on Care and Justice* (New York: Teachers College Press, 2004), xi.

189 *Many white students pride themselves on being colorblind*: I have found this to be true in my conversations with students. See also Casey, "Living with Difference," 40.

The importance of understanding race for black adolescents: See, for example, Janie Ward, *The Skin We're In: Teaching Our Teens to Be Emotionally Strong, Socially Smart, and Spiritually Connected* (New York: Free Press, 2002).

Black kids' self-esteem as high or higher than white students: See Roy Baumeister, Laura Smart, and Joseph Boden, "Relation of Threatened Egotism to Violence and Aggression: The Dark Side of High Self-Esteem," *Psychological Review* 103, no. 1 (1996): 6. See also S. Shirley Feldman and Glen R. Elliott, eds., *At the Threshold: The Developing Adolescent* (Cambridge, MA: Harvard University Press, 1990), 369.

King on being "extremists for love": Martin Luther King Jr., "Letter from Birmingham Jail," April 16, 1963, http://www.mlkonline.net/jail.html.

African Americans place a high premium on respect and black children more likely to defer to their parents and other authorities: M. S. King, "Ethnic Variations in Interpersonal Styles: Investigating Developmental and Cultural Themes in African American, White and Latino Students' Social Competence" (doctoral thesis, Harvard University, 2007), 8.

190 *Research indicating that black families emphasize perseverance in the
face of adversity:* Nancy Hill and Kevin Bush, "Relationships Between
Parenting Environment and Children's Mental Health among African American and European American Mothers and Children," *Journal of Marriage and Family* 63 (November 2001): 956.

*Black parents forceful with their kids while also communicating
warmth:* See, for example, Jeanne Brooks-Gunn and Lisa B. Mark-
man, "The Contribution of Parenting to Ethnic and Racial Gaps in
School Readiness," *Future of Children* 15, no. 1 (Spring 2005): 148. See
also King, "Ethnic Variations in Interpersonal Styles," 8.

*Black families value both group effort toward common goals and
interdependence and respect for family:* King, "Ethnic Variations in
Interpersonal Styles," 6; Andrew Billingsley, *Black Families and
the Struggle for Survival: Teaching Our Children to Walk Tall* (New
York: Friendship Press, 1974), cited in Hill and Bush, "Relationships Between Parent Environment and Children's Mental Health,"
956.

Black adults more willing to confront children with hard realities: Audrey Thompson, "Caring and Color Talk: Childhood Innocence
in White and Black," in Walker and Snarey, *Race-ing Moral Formation,* 33.

*Strong cultural norms in black communities that prohibit pushing for-
ward one's own children:* Walker and Snarey, *Race-ing Moral Formation,* 11.

192 *Research suggesting many low-income and working-class families
maintain authority, praise less, and expect good behavior:* See, for example, Vonnie C. McLoyd, "The Impact of Economic Hardship on
Black Families and Children," 322: see also, Annette Lareau, *Unequal
Childhoods.*

193 *White teachers seeing "what the children see":* Audrey Thompson,
"Caring and Color Talk," in Walker and Snarey, *Race-ing Moral Formation,* 37.

*Parents and teachers still trying to teach children to simply be color-
blind:* Mica Pollock argues that many parents and teachers are struggling with whether or not to try to teach children to be colorblind
and that some teachers are telling children that to notice race is itself
racist. Personal communication with Mica Pollock, 2008, and *Color-
mute: Race Talk Dilemmas in an American School* (Princeton, NJ:
Princeton University Press, 2004). See also Beverly Tatum, "Color
Blind or Color Conscious?," School Administrator, May 1999.

Conclusion: Moral Communities

196 *Kagan on the culture promoting self-interest:* Personal communication with Jerome Kagan, 2007.

Research suggesting that parents are reluctant to interfere in the lives of other families even when they suspect a neighbor of abusing a child: Steve Farkas, with Jean Johnson, *Kids These Days: What Americans Really Think About the Next Generation* (New York: Public Agenda, 1997), 26.

197 *Gallup Poll on perception of the country's moral state and Halberstam's observation that this perception can lower moral expectations:* Joshua Halberstam, "Right and Wrong in the Real World," *Greater Good* 3, no. 1 (2006): 6.

198 *Students' belief that successful people cheat:* Joan Vennochi, "Reading, Writing, and Cheating," *Boston Globe,* September 20, 2007, citing a report by the Josephson Institute of Ethics, Los Angeles.

Philip Rieff on counting "satisfactions and dissatisfactions": Rieff said this fifty years ago. He was marking the arrival of a new type of person whom he called "psychological man." Quoted in Elisabeth Lasch-Quinn, "The Mind of the Moralist," *New Republic,* August 28, 2006, 28.

199 *Research on caretaking fathers' positive moral influences:* Richard Koestner, Carol Franz, and Joel Weinberger, "The Family Origins of Empathic Concern: A 26-Year Longitudinal Study," *Journal of Personality and Social Psychology* 58, no. 4 (1990): 710. See in particular this cited article: Eldred Rutherford and Paul Mussen, "Generosity in Nursery School Boys," *Child Development* 39 (1968): 755–65.

James May on healthcare professionals focusing on mothers: Unpublished study by May, former director of the Fathers Network (http://www.fathersnetwork.org). May reported these results in a personal communication, 2007.

200 *Employers should make workplaces more father-friendly:* For insights on how workplaces can become more father-friendly, see James Levine and Todd Pittinsky, *Working Fathers: New Strategies for Balancing Work and Family* (Reading, MA: Addison-Wesley, 1997).

202 *William Damon on youth charters:* William Damon, *The Youth Charter: How Communities Can Work Together to Raise Standards for All Our Children* (New York: Free Press, 1997).

206 *Faulkner quote:* Cited in William Bennett, "What Really Ails America," in *The McGraw-Hill Reader: Issues Across the Disciplines,* ed. Gilbert H. Muller (Boston: McGraw-Hill Higher Education, 2000), 345.